STUDIES IN ENGLISH LITERATURES

Edited by Koray Melikoğlu

Paola Baseotto

"Disdeining life, desiring leaue to die"

Spenser and the Psychology of Despair

STUDIES IN ENGLISH LITERATURES

Edited by Koray Melikoğlu

ISSN 1614-4651

1   *Özden Sözalan*
The Staged Encounter
Contemporary Feminism and Women's Drama
2nd, revised editon
ISBN 3-89821-367-6

2   *Paul Fox (ed.)*
Decadences
Morality and Aesthetics in British Literature
ISBN 3-89821-573-3

3   *Daniel M. Shea*
James Joyce and the Mythology of Modernism
ISBN 3-89821-574-1

4   *Paul Fox and Koray Melikoğlu (eds.)*
Formal Investigations
Aesthetic Style in Late-Victorian and Edwardian Detective Fiction
ISBN 978-3-89821-593-0

5   *David Ellis*
Writing Home
Black Writing in Britain Since the War
ISBN 978-3-89821-591-6

6   *Wei H. Kao*
The Formation of an Irish Literary Canon in the Mid-Twentieth Century
ISBN 978-3-89821-545-9

7   *Bianca Del Villano*
Ghostly Alterities
Spectrality and Contemporary Literatures in English
ISBN 978-3-89821-714-9

8   *Melanie Ann Hanson*
Decapitation and Disgorgement
The Female Body's Text in Early Modern English Drama and Poetry
ISBN 978-3-89821-605-5

9   *Shafquat Towheed (ed.)*
New Readings in the Literature of British India, c.1780-1947
ISBN 978-3-89821-673-9

Paola Baseotto

"DISDEINING LIFE, DESIRING LEAUE TO DIE"

Spenser and the Psychology of Despair

ibidem-Verlag
Stuttgart

Bibliografische Information der Deutschen Nationalbibliothek
Die Deutsche Nationalbibliothek verzeichnet diese Publikation in der
Deutschen Nationalbibliografie; detaillierte bibliografische Daten sind im
Internet über http://dnb.d-nb.de abrufbar.

Bibliographic information published by the Deutsche Nationalbibliothek
Die Deutsche Nationalbibliothek lists this publication in the Deutsche Nationalbibliografie;
detailed bibliographic data are available in the Internet at http://dnb.d-nb.de.

Cover illustration:
Malincolia. From *Iconologia*, by Cesare Ripa, vol. IV, p. 70, 1766. First publ. in 1593 without illustrations. Keio University Library, JAPAN.

∞

Gedruckt auf alterungsbeständigem, säurefreien Papier
Printed on acid-free paper

ISSN: 1614-4651

ISBN-10: 3-89821-567-9
ISBN-13: 978-3-89821-567-1

© *ibidem*-Verlag
Stuttgart 2008

Alle Rechte vorbehalten

Das Werk einschließlich aller seiner Teile ist urheberrechtlich geschützt. Jede Verwertung außerhalb der engen Grenzen des Urheberrechtsgesetzes ist ohne Zustimmung des Verlages unzulässig und strafbar. Dies gilt insbesondere für Vervielfältigungen, Übersetzungen, Mikroverfilmungen und elektronische Speicherformen sowie die Einspeicherung und Verarbeitung in elektronischen Systemen.

All rights reserved. No part of this publication may be reproduced, stored in or introduced into a retrieval system, or transmitted, in any form, or by any means (electronic, mechanical, photocopying, recording or otherwise) without the prior written permission of the publisher. Any person who does any unauthorized act in relation to this publication may be liable to criminal prosecution and civil claims for damages.

Printed in Germany

For Roberto, my "sweetest sweet" (*Faerie Queene* 3.4.39.8)

Contents

Acknowledgements	xi
Note on Texts	xii
Preface by Elizabeth Heale	xiii
Introduction	1

I. CLASSICAL AND CHRISTIAN ATTITUDES TO MORTALITY — 9
   0. Preface — 9
   1. The Legacy of Classical Philosophies of Life and Death — 12
   2. The Christian Paradox of Life and Death — 19

II. THE PSYCHOLOGY OF DESPAIR: THE DEATH-WISH AND THE LIVING DEATH MOTIFS IN *THE FAERIE QUEENE* — 29
   3. The Desire for Death — 29
   4. Christian Death-Wish and Weariness of Life — 36
   5. Death as Escape from Suffering — 75
   6. Living Death and Deathless Life — 84
   7. The Living Death of the "Old Man" — 89

III. BEREAVEMENT AND ELEGY — 97
   8. The Formal and Thematic Orthodoxy of "November" — 97
   9. *Daphnaida*: An Unconventional Elegy — 109

IV. THE SIGHT OF RUINS AND THE "SABAOTHS SIGHT" — 137
   10. Melancholy and Complaints — 137
   11. Colin's "Worldly Sorow" (2 Cor. 7.10) — 142
   12. Fleshly and Spiritual Views of the *Ruines of Time* — 147
   13. Perspectives on Mutabilitie — 158

Bibliography 167
– Primary Sources 167
– Secondary Sources 170
Index 179

Acknowledgements

The writing of this book and the research leading to it was made possible by the award of a research grant from IULM University. I am grateful to Patrizia Nerozzi Bellman and Anna Busi. My research profited from many stimulating conversations with Tim Parks and Edoardo Zuccato of IULM University.

This book was originally conceived as a doctoral thesis at the University of Reading. I owe a lifelong debt of gratitude to my supervisor Elizabeth Heale for the copious time and scrupulous attention she gave to this project. My work has benefited enormously from her criticism, wisdom and encouragement. It has been a privilege to work with someone who is not only a thoughtful critic and a superb teacher, but a very special person as well. I wish to thank my examiners, Christopher Hardman of Reading University and Richard McCabe of Merton College, Oxford, for offering constructive criticism. Special thanks to Koray Melikoğlu who gave me the opportunity to contribute to the *ibidem* series "Studies in English Literatures." He has proved to be a supporting and welcoming editor.

While I was revising the present work for publication, my husband and I went through very hard times. We are very grateful to the many people who were close to us. Our gratitude goes to Professors Paolo Pederzoli and Claudio Bassi, both wonderful doctors and extremely warm and generous men. Very special thanks to Francesca and Alessandro Mazzucco.

A great debt of gratitude is to my brother Franco.

Note on texts

- Quotations from *The Faerie Queene* are from the 1977 edition by A. C. Hamilton. Longman Annotated English Poets. London and New York: Longman, 1977.
- Quotations from all other Spenserian works are from *The Works of Edmund Spenser: A Variorum Edition*. Ed. E. A. Greenlaw, F. M. Padelford, C. G. Osgood, et al. 10 vols. Baltimore: Johns Hopkins University Press, 1932-1949.
- I have also used the following annotated editions of *The Faerie Queene*, the *Mutabilitie Cantos* and the shorter poems:
  - *The Faerie Queene*. Ed. A. C. Hamilton. London: Longman, 2001
  - *The Mutabilitie Cantos*. Ed. Sheldon P. Zitner. London: Nelson, 1968
  - *The Shorter Poems*. Ed. Richard McCabe. London: Penguin, 1999
  - *The Yale Edition of the Shorter Poems of Edmund Spenser*. Ed. William A. Oram, Einar Bjorvand, Ronald Bond, Thomas H. Cain, Alexander Dunlop, Richard Schell. New Haven: Yale University Press, 1989
  - *Complaints*. Ed. William L. Renwick. London: Scholartis, 1928.
- Quotations from the Bible are from the Geneva version in the edition of 1597. London: Christopher Barker.
- Quotations from William Shakespeare are from *The Complete Works*. Ed. Stanley Wells, Gary Taylor, John Jowett, and William Montgomery. Oxford: Clarendon Press, 1988.

Preface

Death is everywhere in Spenser's works, from the *ubi sunt* theme of his first printed work in the *Theatre of Worldlings* to the anticipation of "that Sabaoths sight" in the last fragmentary words of *The Faerie Queene*. On one occasion only he appears in person, in the Garden of Adonis in Book 3 of *The Faerie Queene*, a composite figure of Time and the Angel of Death, with scythe and "flaggy winges," cutting down and by so doing renewing, the endless forms of life. Paola Baseotto's important study of death and its significance across the full range of Spenser's work allows us to see this ambiguous figure of death in the Garden of Adonis as both typical and unusual. While the ambiguity of death as a force of good and ill, and its intimate linking with life through time are shown in this study to be thoroughly characteristic, the technique of personification, casting death as an object detached from human agency proves highly unusual.

Baseotto's study stresses death's ubiquity as a concept in Spenser's works, always present in intimate relation to life, whether in the recurring, disturbing, figures of "deathwishers," characters who seem to belong as much to the dead as the living, or as a perspective, challenging both characters and readers, to reassess their own apprehension of death and the way in which it shapes our lives. Baseotto's analyses of Spenser's "deathwishers" and "living dead," whether Redcrosse confronting his alter ego Despair, the ghastly Maleger, the Frankenstein-like bodily resurrection of Sansjoy, or the figure of Alcyon trapped in his grief in *Daphnaida*, focus our attention on some of the most compelling and distinctive images in Spenser's work, illuminating our understanding of their power and significance through a combination of detailed attention to language and context, and a thoroughly informed understanding of contemporaneous religious ideas and attitudes.

Spenser proves to be theologically both orthodox and unusual, focussing less on the spiritual and moral dangers of fear of death than those of fear of life. Baseotto stresses the unusual sympathy of Spenser's writing for those weary of life, even such "living dead" as the grotesque and despairing Malbecco, feeding endlessly on his own fears. For Baseotto, Death is absolutely central to understanding Spenser's moral teaching: only the right apprehension of death can produce the freedom to live life well. Through close and sensitive study of Spenser's writing from *The Shepheardes Calender*, through *The Faerie Queene*, to such little discussed poems as *The Ruines of Time* and *Daphnaida* in *Complaints*, Baseotto establishes the centrality, the subtlety and the distinctiveness of Spenser's figuring of death. Her study offers us a new and illuminating understanding of an aspect of Spenser's writing that is fundamental, but which has been strangely neglected in recent decades.

Elizabeth Heale
University of Reading

Introduction

A look at the bibliography of Spenser scholarship found in *The Spenser Review* gives an idea of the emphases of Spenserian studies in recent years.[1] Spenser's active commitment in practical politics in Ireland has been the subject of considerable interest. Gender-conscious studies have engaged with the complex and often contradictory Spenserian representations of the private and public roles of female characters. The ambiguities of Spenserian treatments of his Queen, of her policies, and of the weaknesses inherent in her private body are also receiving the attention they deserve. In recent years there has also been a relative flurry of interest in Spenser's use of British history and the epic medium in his effort to revisit and re-create a British mythical past, and announce future glories. A subject that in my view receives great emphasis throughout Spenser's work, and deserves thorough discussion, that of death, has so far received little attention.[2] While some aspects of death in relation to single episodes or works have been discussed, no attempt has been made to look across the entire canon to trace common patterns that recur in Spenser's texts, nor has the poetic and ideological relevance of the theme of death in all his writing been discussed.[3]

---

[1] See *The Spenser Review*, especially 31.3 (Autumn 2000) and 33.3 (Autumn 2002). *The Spenser Review* offers yearly updates on the bibliography of Spenser studies.

[2] As Bellamy, Cheney, and Schoenfeldt point out, "a MLA database search on Spenser and death turns up very little" (93). Amazingly, the *Spenser Encyclopedia*, that valuable companion to Spenser scholarship, has no specific entry on death. Indeed, the topic of death is central in Renaissance studies. The list of excellent social and cultural histories of death is very long and includes influential works by Ariès, Cressy, Dollimore, Gittings, Gordon and Marshall, Houlbrooke, Neill, Stein and Watson.

[3] Apart from a discussion of themes related to death in *A View of the Present State of Ireland*, *Epithalamion* and *Prothalamion* in "Anatomizing death," the three essays on Spenser and the three essays on Spenser and Milton in the most recent treatment of the topic of death in Spenser, *Imagining Death in*

Death is omnipresent in the Spenserian canon, both in its visible manifestations and as an invisible principle that shapes attitudes to life and its significance. In Spenser's work death is multi-faceted, represented as good, but also as cruel, as a blessing to some, to others a curse. Nearly every violent way of dying is dramatized, from death in war, to suicide, to murder, and every meaning of death is examined, from death as punishment of the wicked, to death as new birth. Among the themes explored in relation to death are justice and vengeance, the contrasting perspectives of earth and heaven, mutability, and decay.

It is my contention, however, that what makes the motif of death in Spenser's works distinctive is not merely its pervasiveness or the remarkable variety of ways in which it is treated. It is rather the way in which death becomes a crucial test of the moral and spiritual condition of his characters. The entire Spenserian canon, not just his major poem, seems to me aimed at fashioning readers in "vertuous and gentle discipline" (*Faerie Queene*, "A Letter of the Authors") and central to the definition of virtue, I suggest, is an approved psychological and spiritual understanding of the significance of death.

Spenser's use of the term 'discipline' is rich in meanings and implications. While 'discipline' in Spenser's work is, according to the *Oxford English Dictionary*, certainly also understood as "mental and moral training," it is above all an "instruction having for its aim to form the pupil to proper conduct and action" (3.a). It points to the spiritual, ethical and social responsibilities of the individual faced with the complexities of earthly experience. The gentleman Spenser's work aims at fashioning, in fact, is clearly no contemplative, no hermit or wise man watching worldly affairs from an ivory tower. Repeatedly, the heroes of Spenser's works are those who take an active part in worldly business, who find their place within the natural cycle, and learn to accept but not precipitate the limits of human life. Submission to the various "disciplines" of death is a yardstick for virtuous living

---

Spenser and Milton, ed. Bellamy, Cheney, and Schoenfeldt, concentrate on *The Faerie Queene*.

in this world. We see this in depictions of violent death where the legitimacy and restraint of violence are presented as crucial when inflicting death on others. We see it in relation to suicide, and more generally in the desire to free the self from the suffering and imperfection of life caused by bereavement and sin. In such circumstances, to seek death by the wrong means or with the wrong attitude is to transform death as access to new life, into the death of the soul. I argue that death is such a crucial concept in Spenser's work because as well as being, as I have suggested, a litmus test of virtue, it is liminal between this fleshly world and the spiritual world. In a sense, death is the "veil" that all Spenser's writing strives to be, belonging to this world but pointing to the truths of the next. Death breaks down the veil of language and of fleshly perceptions, but in doing so it precipitates us into silence. We can only imagine what lies beyond it through fictions and imaginations which still partake of language and fleshly perceptions.

The present study organizes itself as a discovery and exploration of significant areas of "a largely undiscovered country, from whose bourn few travelers return," viz, the theme of death in Spenser's work.[4] My close readings of relevant texts throughout the entire Spenserian canon in the context of traditional and contemporary theological, medical, and moral discourses of death, allow me, I believe, to differentiate unusual emphases from commonplace ideas and to gauge the singularity or the orthodoxy of Spenserian treatments of death. In fact, I will argue that Spenser's perspectives are often strikingly distinctive.

If violent death is a conspicuous motif especially in the *Faerie Queene* and in *A View of the Present State of Ireland*, both in the epic and in the rest of the Spenserian canon, however, death is omnipresent in less physical but no less powerful forms. It is there both as a destructive and as a creative force that through its agents, time and mu-

---

[4] I use Patrick Cheney's evocative description of the topic of death in Spenser's writings ("Dido to Daphne" 143).

tability, brings at the same time individual loss and universal gain, by causing the annihilation of individuals and making the continuation of life possible. My aim in the present study is an exploration of Spenser's view of death as not merely the end of life, but something intertwined with its very core. I shall try and show how death is a central issue in Spenser's texts and I shall argue that his distinctive emphasis falls on the motif of the loss of will to live. In fact, Spenser's work, a work pervaded by melancholy and bitter reflections on the toil and suffering inherent in the human condition, abounds in fictions of characters who invoke death as a deliverance from life.

Death pervades Spenser's texts not as a horrible and frightful presence as in most contemporary writings, but as a mirage, a temptation, an alternative to engagement. The theme of death in Spenser's work is closely intertwined with the Spenserian motif par excellence, that of the quest. His narratives of death emphasize the difficulties of any quest, that of the just man, that of the Christian knight, that of the individual immersed in the flux of change. In texts that promote the virtues of dutiful endurance, there is a repeated dramatization of the temptation to disengage in order to shun the frustration of finding that earthly harvest is but "a weedye crop of care" (*Shepheardes Calender*, "December" 122) and be spared further suffering since "griefe / Well seemes t'exceede the powre of patience" (*FQ* 3.11.14).

While Spenser shares the contemporary preoccupation with mortality as a postlapsarian force conditioning the whole span and all aspects of life, what is distinctive in his own approach to this major concern is his emphasis on the link between mortality and human suffering. Whereas Elizabethan churchmen, philosophers and poets focused mainly on the function of mortality, the first describing it as a constant reminder of the falleness of both humanity and the world and a warning against immoderate attachment to ephemera, the second highlighting the crucial role mortality plays together with the other laws of nature within an ordered universe, and the last underlining how mortality makes earthly goods seem more desirable in their regrettable transience, Spenser focuses mainly on the effects of mortality on people, their psychology and view of life. He concentrates on the consequences in terms of suffering of the perception of death's omnipresence in life. Hence the melancholy arising from the awareness of universal ephemerality, the sense of disillusion and exhaustion following abortive quests and the toilsome erection of material and immaterial monuments that fall to pieces, the inconsolable grief of the bereaved, and an ever frustrated longing for stability and permanence, are recurrent and conspicuous motifs in Spenser's work.

Spenser creates fictions in which various characters are confronted with various types of losses: loss of loved ones, patrons, possessions, positions, hope, confidence in one's power to create anything permanent. In such circumstances, many Spenserian characters react by manifesting a loss of will to live that is very much a desire to be spared future losses. In fact, numerous narratives in Spenser centre on their protagonists' disheartenment and weariness with, and even loathing of, life. These narratives that feature characters who declare themselves unwilling to live, who bear impatiently a suffering that Spenser everywhere represents as the rule and not the exception in this life, and who entreat death to come and obliterate a life they see as a living death, are noteworthy both for their recurrence and dramatic quality.

While the writings of Elizabethan moralists and philosophers abound in suggestions about how to live well and how to view life from the perspective of its end, and while literary works are often pervaded by a sense of regret for life's brevity, from the Spenserian texts there emerges an apprehension of life's excessive duration and death's delay. Indeed, whereas horror and fear of death, together with a rich store of rational and theological arguments aimed at dispelling such fears, are at the centre of the classical and Christian discourses of death that shape Renaissance views (see Part I below), in Spenser's work the emphasis lies elsewhere. It is life, not death that appears to many of his characters as a frightful and painful trial, and therefore it is often fascination with death, rather than attachment to life, that they find nearly irresistible.

While the Christian framework of Spenser's narratives points to a view of death as a blessing, as the door into eternity and the source of new life, his characters often crave death as a welcome destroyer. The impulse to discard one's sinful and suffering self together with the world that disappoints one's expectations is represented as a pervasive temptation throughout Spenser's canon. Living in "liues despight" (*FQ* 2.1.36), loathing their vulnerable and corruptible selves, many Spenserian characters feel imprisoned in a living death or deathless life. Unlike the protagonists of the *artes moriendi*, Spenser's characters are often on the point of yielding to despair while they strive to endure the pangs not of death, but of life. For them, it is life that is the painful thing to face, not death. Indeed, the crucial fight against despair in Spenser is fought not in the face of death, but in the face of life. In this light, an *ars vivendi*, rather than an *ars moriendi* is what is needed and this, I argue, Spenser offers in his narratives of death.

Undoubtedly, Spenser's texts are particularly eloquent on the theme of human vulnerability to, and resentment of, the limitations and suffering inherent in the condition of living in a mutable world. If his treatment of the themes of mutability, decay, and transitoriness is extremely effective, but still utterly conventional, he sounds a more distinctive note when he dramatizes the psychology of despair. He creates fictions that compare fleshly and spiritual views of and responses to life and death. In his narratives the merely earthbound perspective renders the suffering and loss inherent in mortal life meaningless and purposeless. When his characters lose sight of the perspectives of faith, they fall prey to despair, failing to grasp the significance of events within the context of God's providential scheme.

Spenser's narratives suggest that if impatience and despair are understandable responses to the tribulations of mortal life, they ultimately arise from a very limited view of the true dimension and direction of earthly life. The more people look for fulfilment, permanence and stability in the here and now, the more they expose themselves to disillusionments that easily arouse despair. In *Faerie Queene* 1.10 Contemplation shows Redcrosse that toil and suffering, being part of the burden fallen mortals have to bear on their way to heaven, are inescapable on earth. Protests against one's share in the common lot of mortals or attempts at penetrating the mystery of human suffering are therefore irrational, impious and vain. In the *Mutabilitie Cantos* faith in the final transfiguration of all that is mortal and mutable is the only bulwark against despair. The "new man" is one who stops looking for a solution to the mystery of human suffering and looks forward to its annihilation in the afterlife when permanence will take the place of impermanence, bliss of sorrow, true life of living death.

The underlying motif that links a great number of Spenserian narratives of death is the simultaneous implicit censure of fleshly views that emerges from the Christian context of his work, and a pervasive sympathy for the plight of those who hold such views. If the suffering of those in Spenser's work who disconsolately complain about "this worlds vainnesse and lifes wretchednesse" (*Daphnaida* 34) is often described with emotion and sympathy, their blindness and earthliness are nevertheless exposed, as the context makes it clear that as Christians they should not expect happiness and fulfilment from this life. Their death-desire is contrasted with an intense, holy longing for the continuation of life after death. The hateful sight of ruins disappears only when the "Sabaoths sight" (*FQ* 7.8.2) transfigures it.

I
Classical and Christian Attitudes to Mortality

0. Preface

> Innumerable are the evils that beset human life; innumerable, too, the deaths that threaten it. [. . .] Amid these tribulations must not man be most miserable, since, but half alive in life, he weakly draws his anxious and languid breath, as if he had a sword perpetually hanging over his neck? (Calvin 1: 223)

Calvin's words express very well the early modern sense of death's omnipresence in life, the distressing awareness of life's brevity and the disturbing idea of mortality as the outstanding feature of both the macro- and microcosm. Although certainly not a prerogative of the period, meditation on these issues was particularly frequent and intense at that time. Descriptions of man as "a dead corpse breathing" or "a slave bound face to face to Death," were not manifestations of exceptional pessimism or anxiety, but expressions of a shared point of view (Becon, *Sicke Mannes Salue* 94; Chapman 4.4.38). In fact, a particularly acute obsession with death is usually singled out by scholars as one of the distinctive features of the sixteenth and early seventeenth centuries.[5]

---

[5] Whereas most scholars agree the age was marked by an obsession with death, they tend to hold different opinions as to why it was so. Among others, Philippe Ariès sees intensification of love of earthly things and sadness at the idea of having to leave everything behind, as a likely source of obsessive thoughts on death (*Hour of Our Death* 128-32). Alberto Tenenti holds the same view and shows how Catholic and Protestant churchmen used this feeling to persuade Christians into reforming their lives (30-61). Other scholars such as Lynn White highlight the link between high death rates and obsession with death (26). Ariès has investigated the link between a growing sense of personal identity and fear of death in *Hour of Our Death* (95-139; 409-74; 605-11) and *Western Attitudes toward Death* (27-52). Watson has argued that Protestant theology, by denying the existence of purgatory and hence the efficacy of prayers for the dead and the value of good works or sacramental

This obsession was at least partly fed with observations of contemporary reality: death, in fact, was undoubtedly visible and familiar to an extent we moderns can hardly comprehend. Life expectancy was rather low, infant mortality rates were very high, medicine was powerless to deal even with what we now see as minor diseases, while recurring epidemics, famine and wars constantly increased the number of untimely deaths.[6] Commenting upon statistics, G. W. Pigman remarks that "when Renaissance writers insist that the time of death is every moment, they are not exaggerating" (129). Since people were frequently confronted, often from an early age, with the death of friends and relatives and nothing like the modern hasty removal of the dying and the dead from sight was customary, death and the dead were a fairly habitual sight, making early modern individuals well aware of the immanence and omnipresence of death. This awareness of the impending presence of death in the lives of both young and old often surfaces in poetry and stimulates bitter reflections like Robert Southwell's "And many of my mates are gone, / My youngers daily drop away" ("Upon the Image of Death" 104, lines 32-33).[7]

But death's physical presence in everyday life was not the only stimulus to the constant early modern meditation on it. Humanism contributed to the universal focusing of attention on death, since death figures conspicuously among the subjects dealt with in the rich corpus of classical literary and philosophical writings which the humanists translated, annotated and popularized and which helped shape Renais-

---

helps towards salvation, heightened "the psychological burdens of mortality" (5).

[6] For statistics and general information about the victims of famine, war and disease in the early modern period, see Wrigley and Schofield, *The Population History of England, 1541-1871*, which offers a wealth of data together with illuminating analyses of them.

[7] Becon's *Sicke Mannes Salue* develops the same view of death's phenomenal voracity when Epaphroditus calls his son to his deathbed and addresses him thus: "Of all the sons that God hath given me since I was married to this thy mother, thou alone art left alive" (132).

I Classical and Christian Attitudes to Mortality 11

sance ideas. The "old philosophic theme that life is a meditation on death," certainly not unfamiliar in the Middle Ages, was now emphasized by a wider range of documentary reiteration, much of it drawn from classical texts (Stein 41).[8] In the two following chapters, I shall summarize ideas about death, what happens after death, and concomitant attitudes to virtuous living, in classical pagan and Christian writings available to Spenser before turning to detailed analyses of the complex and distinctive representations of death, and the relationships between death and life, in Spenser's works.

---

[8] Seneca maintained that "preparation for death should come before preparation for life" (letter 61.4; 1: 199).

1. The Legacy of Classical Philosophies of Life and Death

Nothing like the Christian univocal view of death and the afterlife is to be found in classical antiquity. Among the great Greek and Latin schools of thought, opinions regarding these crucial issues differed greatly. Pythagoras (571-496 BC) saw life and death as part of a universal cycle of dissolution and regeneration and formulated the doctrine of the transmigration of souls or metempsychosis.[9] Heraclitus (540-480 BC) held humanity and the world are constantly immersed in a state of flux; to him death and life are one in the circular movement of change. Empedocles (c. 492-432 BC) denied death altogether, since in his view nothing ever ceases to exist within the process of incessant mingling and separation of elements that is life. According to Plato (428/7-348 BC), the immortal soul is released from the prison of the body at death and then, purified through successive incarnations, is led back to its divine source and to contemplation of truth in the World of Ideas. Epicurus (341-271 BC) held the notion of the mutability of forms within permanence of matter; hence in his view new beings are incessantly formed out of that same matter that others shed at death.[10]

No less than views of the significance of life and death within a process of creation, change and dissolution, various classical ideas of the afterlife and responses to death influence later perceptions. The afterlife, when any is imagined and no notion of complete annihilation of body and soul is advanced, as in Lucretius (*De Rerum Natura*, book 3, lines 830-69), is represented in unattractive terms, except in Plato's philosophical and Vergil's poetic depictions of it. Christiane Sourvinou-Inwood has carefully investigated approaches to death and views of the afterlife in ancient Greece. She highlights the tight link between the early Greek picture of the afterlife, the picture found in the Homeric poems, and the generally accepted idea of the process of separa-

---

[9] A version of Pythagoras's doctrine is found in the Garden of Adonis episode, *Faerie Queene* 3.6.

[10] In Spenser's words, "substance is eterne," since when a "forme does fade," matter is "chaunged," not destroyed (*FQ* 3.6.37).

tion taking place at death when the *psyche*, soul or shade, leaves the body to enter Hades. What comes after life is seen as a shadow of it, a sort of survival, a diminished form of existence. Believed to be "witless senseless ghosts" or at best "lively shades," the deceased survive in a shadowy, joyless dimension: they recall the inhabitants of Sheol" (Sourvinou-Inwood 18).[11]

Apart from Plato's view of the return of souls to their divine source,

> the idea of the translation of individual heroes to the 'Islands of the Blest,' and the belief current in 'Orphic' and Pythagorean circles that death is a liberation of the soul imprisoned in the body and the doctrine held in these circles of the transmigration of souls, death counted as the end of life, and accordingly as a thing of terror. (Bultmann 27)[12]

Sourvinou-Inwood sees the well-known episode of Odysseus's encounter with Achilles' shadow in Hades as a dramatization of the widespread view of the deceased as "diminished versions of men" (22). Expressing his nostalgia for life, Achilles declares he would gladly exchange his present pre-eminence over the dead for the humblest station in life (*Odyssey* 11.465 ff.). Given the prospects of a shadowy existence in Hades, the contribution of one's matter to the creation of new forms, a long series of reincarnations, or the uncon-

---

[11] The *OED* defines Sheol as "the abode of the dead or departed spirits, conceived by the Hebrews as a subterranean region clothed in thick darkness, return from which is impossible." Bultmann signals and comments on biblical passages that attest two different beliefs as regards the fate of the dead who were thought to be destined either to dwell in Sheol or survive in a very shadowy state in the grave (10-11). Bultmann's is a very well documented study of classical and scriptural views of life and death.

[12] Greek and Roman philosophers and poets often imagine places where the dead dwell only temporarily. Plato's "aerial meadow," for instance, is a temporal abode for souls waiting to assume new bodies; similarly, souls dwell in the Vergilian "Elysian Fields" for a thousand years before rebirth (both qtd. in Hankins 274).

firmed possibility of the soul's return to its divine source, no wonder expectations were firmly attached to this life despite its evils.

The idea that life is preferable to whatever form of existence is thought to come after it, is dominant in the classical tradition and in the scriptural up to the times of the Maccabees, when belief in resurrection and reunion with God became part of Jewish theology.[13] Hence the insistence on life's brevity, the depiction of death as rapacious, and the melancholic regret for the transience of joys, so often evident in the works of ancient poets and thinkers and Jewish prophets.[14]

"What pleasauntness can there be in life, when, by night and by day, we have to reflect already, even already, we are to die?" Cicero's remark is typical of the perception, widespread in the classical world, of mortality as a fact marring the enjoyment of life and arousing sadness (16). Moreover, mortality as the classical writers saw it does not affect human beings and their lives only; it affects the whole universe. Classical writers transmitted to later ages an elegiac sense of cosmic mortality which emphasized a constant process of degeneration driving the world to dissolution. Joseph J. Mogan argues that pre-Christian philosophical views of the tight link between mutability and mortality helped to generate the "medieval sensibility of change-toward-decay," arousing a melancholic, pessimistic vision of things that was current

---

[13] Sourvinou-Inwood supplies abundant documentary evidence of this bleak view of the afterlife evident in Greek, Roman and Jewish writings (17-25). Mogan traces the progressive penetration of the idea of immortality into Jewish thought as the Bible attests it (31-34).

[14] Quotations might be multiplied almost indefinitely. For example, representative of the bleak classical and scriptural views of the human lot are Catullus's beautiful lines from Carmen 5, "Suns may set and rise again: / For us, when the short light has once set, / Remains to be slept the sleep of one unbroken night" (7) and the bitter reflection in Psalm 39, "Doubtlesse man walketh in a shadow, and disquieteth himselfe in vaine: hee heapeth up riches, and cannot tell who shall gather them."

I Classical and Christian Attitudes to Mortality 15

until the idea of progress prevailed around the mid-seventeenth century (21).

Supporting his analysis by a rich store of documentary evidence, Mogan underlines the centrality of issues such as mortality, mutability, decay and transitoriness in classical literary and philosophical writings. He argues that if melancholy and loathing of the state of things are widely attested, from the texts there also emerges a sense of resignation and final acceptance of the status quo arising from the conviction that everything, including mortality and mutability, is an expression of and accords with the immutable laws of nature.[15] The wisest thing to do, then, is to submit willingly to these laws. The wise man concentrates on how to spend in the best possible way the short span he has been allotted and carefully prepares himself for the regrettable but inevitable event of death.

Any reader of classical literature knows that death is often a major subject; the two related issues that receive the greatest amount of attention are fear of death and exhortations to dispel it.[16] The number of writings aimed at persuading people that fear of death is irrational and training in the art of wise acceptance and right preparation for death necessary, is remarkable. All great thinkers make reference to fear of death in their writings aimed at fashioning the perfectly wise and rational man; as often happens, however, poetic representations impress more vividly. Christiane Sourvinou-Inwood notes how Homer builds an abhorrent image of death by largely employing adjectives that depict it as "black, hateful, bringing bitter grief and long woe" (19). The treatment of some themes related to death by another poet whose work was influential in the Renaissance seems to me particularly representative of views of mortality in major Greek and Latin literary writings. In Carmen 2 Horace conveys the idea of the inevitability of death

---

[15] In this light, Cicero urges people to "rank nothing among evils, which is appointed either by the immortal gods, or nature, the parent of all things" (88).

[16] As Stein remarks, "Aristotle had described the fear of death as the greatest of human fears (*Ethics* 3.6.III5a)" (7).

when he reminds a friend that he, like all that lives and breathes, is "doomed to die." Appropriating the *carpe diem* motif, he then exhorts him to enjoy wine, perfumes and flowers "while Fortune and youth allow, and the dark threads of the Sisters three," since soon he will experience the rapacity of death, "thou art pitiless Orcus' victim," and the sadness of life after death, the "everlasting exile" (113).[17]

If ancient Greek and Roman ideas about images of death were familiar to and influential on Renaissance writers, so too, were classical teachings on the right responses to death. To counteract what they deemed immoderate aversion to death, as well as an inclination to excessively melancholic reflections upon universal impermanence, some philosophers and poets appealed to reason and strength of character. The Epicurean Lucretius (c. 99-55 BC) based his argument against fear of death on his belief in the complete annihilation of body and soul; in book 3 of *De Rerum Natura* (vv. 830-69) he asserts fear of death is irrational: "What has this Bugbear Death to frighten Man, / If souls can die, as well as Bodies can?" Since the dead cannot suffer any longer because they are no more, "What is there left for us in Death to fear?" wonders the poet who died a suicide.[18] Book 1 of Cicero's *Tusculan Questions* is almost entirely dedicated to illustration of why it is wise "either to wish for death, or certainly to desist from fearing it." Whether as passage to the afterlife or annihilation, death is in any case a good:

> For if that last of days brings us not extinction, but change of place, what is there more to be wished? But, if it obliterates and sweeps us away altogether, what is better than to drop asleep amidst the labours of life, and thus close our eyes in the drowse of everlasting slumber? (87)

---

[17] Horace's reference to the afterlife as an "everlasting exile" is representative of the classical inclination to see life as the greatest good. Christian theology, of course, holds exactly the opposite view, deeming earthly life an exile.

[18] I quote from John Dryden's translation of the *De Rerum Natura* as reproduced in *The Oxford Book of Death* edited by Dennis J. Enright (28).

I Classical and Christian Attitudes to Mortality 17

A completely different approach (and a very influential one for later centuries) is that of Plato. He argues that if death means the liberation of the soul from the prison of the body and its return to the World of Ideas, that is, its reunion with truth and God, it should rather be desired than dreaded.[19] Plato puts all of life in the perspective of death, stating that the right philosophical attitude to life is to view it as a preparation for death, a process of progressive liberation of the soul from the body. In this light, "the just life finds its fulfilment in the death for which it has always been striving to prepare" (Bultmann 29). In Plato's view, then, death is both an achievement and the door opening into a new form of life. His ideas lent themselves to easy assimilation into the Christian philosophy of death.

"To complain because some one's dead is to complain because he was a human being; the same terms are binding on all: for him whose lot is to be born, death waits" (Seneca, letter 99.8; 2: 176). These words of Seneca express the idea at the basis of the Stoic approach to death: since death is a natural phenomenon, it is irrational to protest against it or loathe it; like all the laws of nature, the fact of mortality must simply be accepted. Besides, since the Stoics believed that virtue is the only good and vice the only evil, in their view death is really no evil at all. Nothing external to people can affect them: "False Goods and False Evils" according to the sixteenth-century Neostoic philosopher Lipsius, are "such things as are not in vs: And which properlie doe not helpe nor hurte the inner man, that is, the minde" (85).[20]

To the Stoics, then, reason and virtue are the bulwarks against all human fears, particularly the fear of death and of Fortune's blows. Death and Fortune are seen as agents of the divine will and the "truly

---

[19] In the *Phaedo* 114c-d, Plato affirms he does hope the soul survives the body, but adds he does not know for sure whether this is what really happens.

[20] Lipsius (1547-1606) edited Tacitus's *Annals* and *Histories* and all the major philosophical works of Seneca. Founder with Guillaume Du Vair of Renaissance Neostoicism, he aimed at reconciling Stoic and Christian principles. On Lipsius and his influence on Renaissance thought, see Morford and Saunders.

virtuous man [. . .] becomes perfectly identified with or submerged into, the divinity or Providence" (Mogan 27). He learns to will what is inescapable and to cultivate what alone is permanent, that is, virtue, disregarding the illusory goods the world offers. If he feels an illness is weakening his rational faculties or a great woe is endangering his balance, the wise man should remember with Seneca that he holds the keys to his prison (*Letters to Lucilius*, letter 70). He should open it himself the moment he realizes he is about to become an irrational slave to passion.

The Stoic philosophy of detachment from wordly goods and cares and serene acceptance of the state of things, the view of life as a training in virtue, and the apprehension of misfortunes and death as no evils, find their most articulate expression in Boethius's *De consolatione philosophiae*, a work whose influence on Western thought until the late Renaissance can hardly be overestimated.[21] It documents Boethius's perception of human and cosmic life as guided by the divine hand. In this perspective neither Fortune's blows, nor death that drives people and things back to God are to be feared or abhorred. The *De consolatione* "ends with Philosophy's resounding affirmation of the existence of freedom and justice in the universe and her exhortation that men should live according to virtue, in expectation of rewards from the supreme Judge (bk. 5)" (Cherniss 15).

---

[21] Written in 524, the *De consolatione* was translated into English for the first time by King Alfred, then by Chaucer and Queen Elizabeth, among others.

2. The Christian Paradox of Life and Death

The fundamental difference between the many classical and the Christian conceptions of death is that the ancient Greeks and Romans saw death as an event happening in accordance with the universal laws of nature, while Christian theology views death as something not created at the beginning, but introduced later as a punishment.[22] No longer seen as a regrettable but natural event in no way linked to ideas of culpability or personal responsibility, death, in the Christian perspective, appears as the most terrible among the consequences of Adam's fault, the expression *par excellence* of God's wrath towards humans, a constant reminder of humanity's inherited corruption and loss of prelapsarian bliss. Joseph J. Mogan argues that this idea of mortality as a punishment for sin is the main source of a widespread Christian pessimism (Chapter 1).

The significance Christian theology attaches to death is nonetheless not univocal. A penalty for the Fall, death is simultaneously a beneficial event, since through Christ's coming and sacrifice it has become the door into life eternal. These two faces of death, one horrible, the other beautiful, its dual nature as the most dreadful punishment and the greatest boon, make the Christian discourse on death and life complex and often contradictory. Hence there is a tension in religious writings between the simultaneous prescriptions to meditate daily on "that uglesome thing," death, which was "brought in by such a thing [sin] so hated of God," (Latimer 1: 220) while also being grateful for the "commodities" it offers.[23] We find both exhortations to fight attachment to an earthly life that is, rightly considered, death, and warnings

---

[22] In *The City of God*, 13.15, Augustine argues that death is not natural (that is to say not ordained by the law of nature), because God has not created death together with the universe. There are countless scriptural references to death as punishment of Adam's sin and Bultmann offers a useful list (44).

[23] I borrow from the title of one of John Bradford's "Godly Meditations vppon the ten commaundementes" (1567) in *Sermons and Meditations*, "A Meditation of Death, and the commodities it bringeth."

that desire for the next life should be great although kept within bounds lest it turns into an unholy death-wish.

These tensions and attempts at the reconciliation of opposites are well documented in Christian writings of all times and places. However, since my main aim at present is to investigate the ideas of death readily available to Spenser, I have selected quotes from widely read works by influential Protestant churchmen of his day.

The paradoxical nature of death is evident in William Perkins's statement that "Death in its owne nature is a Curse, or fore-runner of condemnation, the very gates and suburbs of hell it selfe: but being qualified by Christ, it is a blessing" (*Whole Treatise* 2: 36). As for the tensions inherent in Christian views of earthly life, Calvin often highlights the difference between a holy contempt of life and an immoderate loathing of it that may lead to impatience at its duration. Having listed the evils that afflict body and soul during life in a world that is nothing but a "sepulcher," he concludes "it is still fitting for us to be so affected either by weariness or hatred of it [life] that, desiring its end, we may also be prepared to abide in it at the Lord's pleasure [. . .]." Hence the Christian is asked to "burn with the zeal of death," and at the same time wait patiently for it, as death will come "whenever it shall please the Lord" (Calvin 1: 716). This attitude certainly presupposed great faith and psychological balance.

According to theologians, an excessive and impatient haste to leave earthly corruption behind and gain celestial bliss was not the only attitude that could make people incline more towards an unholy death-wish than a godly desire of death. Churchmen, as their works document, often worried about unholy death-wishes arising from mere exhaustion, self-hatred and loathing of one's condition as a vulnerable mortal. Redcrosse clearly experiences such a death-wish in his encounter with Despair in Book 1 of *The Faerie Queene*, and, as I will show, many Spenserian death-wishers display similar feelings. The constant reiteration from the pulpit and on paper of the utter corruption and filthiness of human beings, the ephemerality and vanity of earthly goods and affections, and the painfulness of life, was ultimately meant to stimulate a godly desire of the next life, but clearly had a less positive effect on some people, contributing to their disheartenment.[24] It is easy to see how the godly attitude of detachment from the world could easily degenerate into an ungodly rejection of the world.

However, judging by the recurrence of the theme and the emphasis it receives in the most popular religious works, churchmen in Spenser's day held that immoderate love of life and the world was more widespread and endangered spiritual wholesomeness more seriously than excessive haste to leave for Heaven. Hence religious advice literature abounds in depreciations of earthly life aimed at persuading people to overcome their attachment to it. One finds countless variations on the idea that "all things in this world be subject unto vanity, yea, they themselves are mere vanity" (Becon, *Jewel of Joy* 474). People are constantly reminded that eternal damnation is the price one pays for the enjoyment of ephemeral pleasures: "the end of all wordly joy, of all carnal pleasure, of all temporal felicity is bitter sorrow and grievous pain" (474).

The *contemptus mundi* motif is an invention neither of Renaissance theology, nor of the Middle Ages. It is traceable to scriptural representations of "all the works that are done under the sunne" as "vanitie, and vexation of the spirit" (Ecclesiastes 1.14). Another crucial source of disparaging apprehensions of earthly life is Plato's view of the dichotomy between material and immaterial, temporal and eternal worlds. It is precisely when the existence of an eternal realm of immutability and permanence is postulated and becomes a touchstone that the apprehension of this world's subjection to change and decay inten-

---

[24] For an appreciation of the recurrence of such themes in devotional literature, see the *General Index to the Publications of the Parker Society* (1855), the very detailed index of names cited and topics discussed in the forty volumes of the Parker Society edition of the writings of the most influential early theologians of the Church of England, under the headings "Man," "World," "Affliction," and "Tribulation."

sifies. Classical philosophy (not just Platonism, but Stoicism, Neo-Platonism and Gnosticism, all of which reflected on life's evils) had sown the seed of pessimism which Christianity, by putting original sin at the core of its theology and stressing people's culpability since birth and their misery, transformed into a leafy tree.[25]

Aware that emphasis on postlapsarian corruption could lead Christians to despair and excessive loathing of this life, the early Fathers never forgot to underline the unique dignity of human beings created in God's own image and the beauty of the universe.[26] But this balancing outlook was to be progressively abandoned in the Middle Ages producing a very bleak view of life unmitigated by more optimistic considerations. It is then that religious writings focusing on contempt of earthly life multiply, their language becomes harsher and their imagery macabre.[27] Works belonging to the *contemptus mundi* genre provide collections of disheartening maxims that develop views of this world as a land of exile. Earthly pleasures pose a threat to people's psychological and spiritual wholesomeness, since their ephemerality exposes people to the experience of loss, and, in indulging in them, people sin. The maxims also reiterate the view that human beings, however beautiful or powerful, are nothing but food for worms.[28]

---

[25] Mogan accurately traces the source of the ideas at the base of the Christian *contemptus mundi* tradition to classical antiquity, then follows their evolution and manipulation in later ages (Chapter 1).

[26] Donald R. Howard gives an account of Augustine's explanation of the fact that "the world could seem so bad and still be the creation of a god who is good. If God is good, Augustine reasoned, all that he creates must be good. But obviously no creature could be as good as God himself; so Augustine called God the immutable Good and his whole creation a mutable good" (52).

[27] On religious works on the *contemptus mundi* and their background, see Robert Bultot's amply documented study *La doctrine du mépris du monde en Occident, de Saint Ambroise à Innocent III*.

[28] The most popular work belonging to the *contemptus mundi* genre (judging by the number of manuscripts, almost 500, and of allusions to it in other writings) was *De miseria humanae conditionis*, written in 1195 by Cardinal

I Classical and Christian Attitudes to Mortality

In order to make their warnings about the dangers inherent in abandoning oneself to wordly pleasures more persuasive, authors of works of contempt did not stop at depreciating earthly life, but anticipated also the horror of damnation and depicted, in often sadistic detail, the physical tortures in hell awaiting those who took this earth for paradise. By doing so, they reinforced the fear of death perceived as being latent in an appreciation of earthly things: "who hateth death," in fact, "but he which loueth life?" (Wright 221). Plinio Prioreschi argues that the old, reassuring view characteristic of early Christian theology of physical death as the passage to a quiet sleep in Abraham's bosom preceding the Second Coming and Last Judgement was supplanted in the Middle Ages by a more unsettling and terrifying vision of the fate of body and soul after the trial of death (87).[29] Medieval moralists and churchmen dwell on the processes of decomposition to make Christians see that the body they nourish with sinful pleasures is really the property of the agents of putrefaction and warn that immediately after death comes individual judgement. Hence a great deal of attention and anxiety focuses on the death-bed, seen as the battlefield where angels and devils struggle for the dying person's soul.[30]

The church certainly played a major role in stimulating fear of death in its attempt to persuade people to moderate their attachment to earthly goods and loves, but it is not solely responsible for the onset or

---

Lotario dei Segni, who later became pope Innocent III. This is a real encyclopedia of pessimistic views of humanity and the world, still widely read in the Renaissance.

[29] One of the scriptural passages that document the early Christian view of what comes immediately after death, is Luke 16.22 where it is said that the dead Lazarus is received in Abraham's bosom.

[30] This attention and anxiety are reflected in the huge number of *artes moriendi* published from the fifteenth century. The most popular and influential sixteenth-century English *artes* were Thomas Becon's *The Sicke Mannes Salue* (1560) and William Perkins's *A Salve for a Sicke Man* (1595). Kathrine Koller gives a useful list of popular sixteenth-century *artes* written or translated into English (130). See also Nancy Lee Beaty's excellent *The Craft of Dying: A Study in the Literary Tradition of the Ars Moriendi in England*.

intensification of that fear. Philippe Ariès has convincingly argued that there is a direct link between the increase in anxiety about death and the establishment of a sense of personal identity (*Western Attitudes toward Death* 27-52; *Hour of Our Death* 138 ff.).[31] While the phenomenon of the rise of individualism is debated, historians of death usually agree in detecting the influence of ideas of identity on views of and responses to death.[32] As the sense of, and attachment to, one's subjectivity intensify, mutability, which first causes the loss of possessions, positions, and loved ones, all constitutive of the self, and then wipes out the self altogether, is likely to be more acutely perceived and loathed. It is easy to see how trust in the intrinsic worth of life and human creative powers, that is, a view of each individual as unique, might provide fertile ground not only for pride and enthusiasm, but also for melancholy.

The link between melancholy and awareness of the transitoriness of all that is earthly is self-evident. Through its agents, mutability and time, mortality holds sway over the world and exposes people to multiple losses. It is because they are ephemeral that all things seem vain and illusory, and as appreciation and attachment to them increase, regret for their impermanence intensifies. Robert Burton, the early seventeenth-century authority on melancholy, traces its source precisely

---

[31] Neill argues that early modern literary and visual representations of death document a growing perception of death as "a cancellation of personal identity [. . .] a condition of dreadful *disfigurement*" (9). See also Dollimore, *Death, Desire and Loss*, especially the chapter on "Death and Identity." Watson highlights the role of the Protestant Reformation with its emphasis on individual interiority in the heightening of the sense of one's subjectivity. In *The Order of Things* Foucault investigates death's conditioning of human life and identity. For a well documented discussion of the establishment of a sense of personal identity, see Alain Laurent's *Histoire de l'individualisme*.

[32] With reference to early modern England, Houlbrooke, *Death, Religion, and the Family* (Chapters 6, 8, 9 and 11) argues that a heightened sense of self led to a new emphasis on individual salvation and survival in the memory of the living signified by changes in the rites of preparation for death, funeral rites and monuments.

to a painful awareness of the lack of permanence of earthly things and human life:

> We are not here as those Angells, celestiall powers and Bodies, Sunne and Moone, to finish our course without all offence, with such constancy, to continue for so many ages: but subject to infirmities, miseries, interrupt, tossed and tumbled up and downe, carried about with every small blast, often molested and disquieted upon each slender occasion, uncertaine, brittle, and so is all that we trust unto. (1: 137)[33]

Melancholy reflections of this kind also abound in Renaissance religious writings and churchmen often deepen the dark tones in which they express such views to persuade people to look away from this world and to contemplate the next. Thomas Becon stigmatizes what to him is immoderate love of life by highlighting both its ungodliness and irrationality:

> Who will trust a life so frail, so transitory, so bond [sic] unto mortality? Who can justly persuade himself to live many years in this world, seeing that in it so suddenly health is turned into sickness, valiance into imbecility, strength into weakness, joy into sadness, comfort into desperation, life into death? *(Sicke Mannes Salue 92)*

Melancholy remarks on the degeneration of the world and warnings about the approaching of the final days also filled Renaissance writings. The world was often represented as upside-down, "out of square" in Spenser's expressive definition (*FQ*, Book 5, proem 1.7), and this seemed to herald the imminence of the end of times, an-

---

[33] Shakespeare says the same in just a few, essential words: "[. . .] in this life / Lie hid more thousand deaths" (*Measure for Measure*, 3.1.39-40). Thomas Wright confirms that melancholy is a universal disease: "[. . .] and few there bee, which are not subject to some melancholy humour, that often assaulteth them, troubling their minds, and hurting their bodies" (62).

nounced by *portenta, signa* and *monstra*. Even a quick survey of chronicles and encyclopedic tracts gives an idea of the general view that witches and horribly deformed newborn babies were to be found everywhere in large numbers.[34] Reports on cosmic perturbations and displacements of planets, sightings of comets and bright crosses in the sky, all seen as signs of the impending end of the world, abound in contemporary miscellaneous writings.[35] Belief in the proximity of the apocalypse, apart from arousing unrestrained feelings of exultation in some particularly pious or fanatic souls, for the majority of people was a further cause of melancholy and anxiety, as it deepened their perception of the transitoriness and brevity of human life.[36]

This synthetic survey of the themes and manifestations of Renaissance pessimism would be incomplete without at least a quick reference to Don Cameron Allen's very interesting opinions about the influence of significant contemporary cultural changes on it. Allen argued that the discovery or rediscovery and assimilation of different philosophical systems not only sometimes at odds one with the other over major issues, but often based on principles that seemed to resist all efforts at reconciliation with Christian thought, had an unsettling effect on people's minds (206-07). The conflictual understanding of the world that ensued served, in Allen's view, to displace Thomism, that old, orthodox and reassuring instrument for interpreting the world.

---

[34] Such a survey is found in Victor Harris, *All Coherence Gone*, section 4.

[35] Stephen Batman, the Anglican minister and author of the most popular sixteenth-century natural history tract, *Batman uppon Bartholome*, writes:
> I therefore [. . .] vppon sight and search of so manye prodigious birthes, Starres of vnaccustomed appearance, enuenomed aires, from which proceede pestilence, plague, war, hunger, frensie, ielousie and heresie, haue no lesse occasion than worthy Authors in former time, to make or set forth this *Chronicle of the Doome, or warning to Gods Iudgement*. (*The Doome*, Dedication)

[36] On apocalyptical expectations and the anxiety caused by a feeling of general degeneration and unsettlement, see Harris, *All Coherence Gone* and Patrides and Wittreich, *The Apocalypse in English Renaissance Thought and Literature*, two seminal and still unsurpassed studies.

I Classical and Christian Attitudes to Mortality 27

Besides philosophy, new discoveries may have offered arguments for pessimism. Allen discusses the exemplary instance of new astronomical observations contradicting the belief in the immutability of the skies: "the observed alterations in the unchanging heavens of Aristotle indicated a decay in an immutable substance, to which man had nailed his faith in the permanent" (212).[37] It is not too difficult to guess the psychological consequences of these new findings on people. The anxiety voiced in Spenser's reflection on the fact that even the sun, "that same glorious lampe of light," "is miscaried with the other spheres" (*FQ*, Book 5, proem 7), is typical of a widespread attitude, for comments of the same kind fill contemporary pages. Cultural change requires a process of adaptation and readjustment and this may well be accompanied by a more or less long period of anxiety and disorientation.[38]

My brief outline of Renaissance views of death shows that themes of mortality and related ideas such as transitoriness and vanity in Spenser's work, however unusual they may be in their emphasis and recurrence, are not exceptional in themselves. As any reader of sixteenth-century writing realizes, Spenser shares a preoccupation with mutability and death with his contemporaries. However, as I shall argue in the following chapter, a single but crucial difference in perspective, evident in Spenser's writings, should not be overlooked. While the picture of death that emerges from the majority of sixteenth-century literary, philosophical, and meditative writings is one of a loathed power that makes life regrettably precarious and substitutes losses for joys (a picture churchmen endeavour to correct by presenting death as the meeting-point between God and human beings), death

---
[37] Mutabilitie's claim to Jove's reign based on the argument that her sway reaches beyond the sublunary world comes to mind here (*FQ* 7.7.49-56).
[38] White describes such a process ("Death and the Devil" 26), and Watson interestingly links it to a particular literary genre: "The rise of Elizabethan and Jacobean tragedy coincides with the emergent scientific view of the universe – a view which necessarily contradicts our narcissism, both as individuals and as species" (9).

for many Spenserian characters appears as an intensely coveted object.[39] If melancholy meditation upon life's brevity is a recurrent item in Renaissance writings, both classical and religious, in Spenser's work it is replaced with reflections on life's unbearably long duration. I will show that Spenser's death-wishers are not champions of Christian resignation to and acceptance of death; their haste to leave the world arises from a fleshly and earthly understanding of the significance of life and death that arouses impatience and a desire for escape. The text evokes a simultaneous sympathy for and censure of those who fall prey to despair because they look at things through the eyes of the "old man" in them.

---

[39] Bishop Hugh Latimer acknowledges that the horror of death is natural and universal, experienced even by the "faithful," "the elect people of God" who, he says, are aware of the fact that death is the ultimate good and "yet for all that, there is nothing that they complain more sore than of this horror of death" (1: 220). Similarly, Calvin admits that "believers, whatever their strength may be, cannot but be frightened by it [death]" (1: 567).

II
The Psychology of Despair: The Death-Wish and the Living Death Motifs in *The Faerie Queene*

3. The Desire for Death

The emphasis in Spenser's work on weariness with life and lust for death does differ significantly from contemporary ideological trends.[40] At a time when the horror of death was fixed on page and canvas, and the *artes moriendi* were produced in great numbers to help Christians prepare for a moment which was seen as painful and dreadful, Spenser presents death as desirable. Very rarely in his work are terms expressing fear, horror or revulsion linked to death, whereas words expressing love, desire, and relief, abound: death is predominantly represented as the ultimate object of human longing, yearned for by both the virtuous and the wicked. It is also remarkable that, unlike most contemporaries, Spenser never dwells on the decay of the body, nor mentions worms, putrefaction and the like. One looks in vain for an equivalent of Shakespeare's or Archbishop George Abbot's grim images of the dead who go "with vilest worms to dwell" (Sonnet 71), "to be amongst worms and vermin" (140).

The theatre frequently exploited the dramatic force and morbid appeal for audiences of the terrifying and horrific aspects of death, and contemporary poetry abounds in melancholic reflections upon human vulnerability to death's rapaciousness.[41] The terrors and horrors linked to death figure conspicuously also in religious writings aimed at reminding people of the mortality and corruption of their physical selves and discouraging excessive attachment to the here and now. However, as we have seen, churchmen often evoke them to show that if fear of

---

[40] In the present chapter I analyse narratives of death-desire in *The Faerie Queene*. The theme however is pervasive also in *Daphnaida* and in the January, June, and December eclogues of the *Shepheardes Calender* which are dealt with in detail in chapters 9 and 11 respectively.

[41] A vast selection of poetic and dramatic treatments of various aspects of death and related themes is found in Enright, *The Oxford Book of Death*.

death is a natural response to death's dreadfulness, Christians should overcome that fear by focusing on the "commodities" death offers.[42] Both in literary and devotional writings then, albeit in different ways and for different purposes, the writing subject assumes an attachment to life and a consequent loathing of death. In Spenser's work, instead, the emphasis is on loathing of life and the consequent desire of death.

Spenser creates many fictions that present sympathetically individual responses to life's hardships which are antithetical to Stoic endurance and Christian patience, the ideals contemporary ideology promoted. Confronted with adversities and losses, many Spenserian characters are impatient, failing to see their own suffering, as the ideology of the sixteenth century suggested they should, as either an opportunity to practice Stoic fortitude, or as the just reward for inherited and personal sins, and thus a stimulus to repentance and reformation. Their responses to trials in terms of despair, loss of will to live and desire of death, show they characteristically view life and death, at least momentarily, from an earthbound point of view from which life seems a meaningless and purposeless series of toils and sorrows that only death as annihilation can interrupt.

Spenser's work offers a large number of single images of despairing individuals, of people experiencing frustration while they labour towards unattainable goals, or of persons annihilated by grief at the death of their hopes and loved ones. Whereas, in general, contemporary complaints dwell on life's brevity, a typical Spenserian complaint conveys the idea of life's excessive and hateful length. While people's tenacious attachment to life worried philosophers and theologians, Spenser's characters such as Redcrosse, Phedon, Pyrochles, and Timias, whose narratives I will analyse, characteristically declare they live unwillingly and passionately entreat death to come soon.

The death-wish in Spenser's work is an unusually pervasive motif. I will argue that Spenser uses it to create fictions that implicitly teach

---

[42] I borrow from the title of one of Bradford's "Godly Meditations," see Chapter 2, footnote 23.

the response to life and death that is proper to the good Christian, by contrasting it with false responses arising from an earthly perspective. In these fictions life appears indeed as nothing but a series of abortive efforts, disillusionment, hardly bearable pain, and death appears as a highly desirable escape from all this. The emphasis in Spenser's work is on the feelings this mortal view arouses: melancholy at the apparent meaninglessness of suffering and a reluctance to accept the sorrows of the human condition.

While, from an earthbound perspective, life may appear as a long, meaningless torture, from the perspective of eternity, everything acquires meaning and direction. This is very explicitly shown in Book 1, canto 10 of *The Faerie Queene*, where the significance of life and death and the right godly response to them are set forth within a fiction of religious initiation and revelation of divine truths through a mystical vision.

As Redcrosse figures forth an Everyman, any Christian striving along the path to holiness, the crucial experience of his illumination in canto 10 is paradigmatical. The importance of the episode can hardly be overestimated: Patrick Grant signals it as the only passage in the *Faerie Queene* "to give a direct glimpse of what the rewards of faithful endurance may be like in the next world" (33). Redcrosse and the reader, however, are reminded that a series of "staggering steps" and "labours long" is between them and the celestial rewards; a "sad delay," life, precedes the enjoyment of "ioyous rest and endlesse blis" (1.10.51, 52). Redcrosse, as the exemplary Christian pilgrim, is told that he should view life as a "painefull pilgrimage" to God's house and be aware that the "path" leading to the "new Hierusalem" is "litle [. . .] both steepe and long" (stanzas 61, 55, 57). As a "man of earth" burdened with a "sinfull soule" (52, 51), he should be aware of his frailty in the face of temptations that expose him to the losses and sufferings that Spenser's texts represent as the rule, not the exception, in this fallen world.

As Redcrosse's paradigmatical experience shows, life is represented as a series of trials: all Christians are likely at some point to get lost in a "wandring wood" (1.1.13) and to follow Redcrosse's erring trajectory through Book 1. All Redcrosse's fighting, suffering, straying, falling, should be recognized as the way in which fallen humans must proceed towards the New Jerusalem. Hardly seen by the elect Christian, immersed in life's troubled waters, it is God's providential hand that drives him there.[43]

The temptations to abandon active life and shun its battles, "here for aye in peace remaine," and to leave the world before the time appointed by God, "streight way on that last long voyage fare" (1.10.63), are presented as understandable, but nonetheless censurable attitudes. Contemplation reminds Redcrosse that the good Christian has to immerse himself in life, go on fighting till his quest is completed and wait patiently for a permanent sight of "things diuine" compared to which "earthly things" are "darke" indeed (1.10.67).

Within the Christian perspective explained by Contemplation, then, life should be viewed as a God-guided progress towards the eternal destination, and its hardships accepted as the inescapable burden of human earthliness and fallenness. Escapism, whether out of loathing for one's lot, or out of desire of "things diuine," should be shunned. From this perspective, all that life brings has sense and purpose; Redcrosse's sins and sufferings contribute to his spiritual growth. They are all part of that Providence-guided pattern that will lead him finally to become the knight of Holiness and then gain access through death to the blessings kept in store for him.

Perhaps more than anything else in Spenser's work, the episode of Redcrosse's vision serves to point the reader in the direction of the Christian perspective and moral purpose that decide his rhetorical strategies. Nowhere else in fact is the dichotomy between terrestrial and celestial perspectives that underpin Spenser's worldview so ex-

---

[43] On the Spenserian dramatization of this view in the *Mutabilitie Cantos*, see Chapter 13 below.

plicitly referred to and visually displayed. In canto 10 a vision of the New Jerusalem is paired with a view of Cleopolis: thus Spenser's narrative features a direct comparison between the Christian's provisional dwelling and his destination. This is the crucial double perspective, explicit here, implied everywhere else in Spenser's poetry, that he expects his reader to keep constantly in view. One should lead a virtuous and productive life in Cleopolis with eyes constantly fixed on the New Jerusalem. In this light, the miseries of this "painefull pilgrimage" should be viewed in the perspective of the joys of the "blessed end" (1.10.61).

Spenserian death-wishers are overwhelmed by despair when they focus on their present condition and fail to keep in mind the promise of its transfiguration. Besides, their main mistake is to expect what cannot be: that the world should be exempt from loss and suffering. From this crucial delusion comes their dismay at life's blows, their loathing of their lot and loss of will to live. Relying too much on the fallen world for their happiness, they despair when their expectations are not met. They forget a crucial scriptural message: God has not promised happiness in the course of earthly life, as Bishop Hugh Latimer put it in an address to his flock, "look for no better cheer as long as thou art in this world: but trouble and vexations thou shalt have *usque ad satietatem*" (1: 436). As Contemplation tells Redcrosse, all God's "Saints" have been as "wretched, and liu'd in like paine" while on earth (1.10.61, 62).

Having fallen prey to exhaustion and despair following various kinds of trials, Spenserian death-wishers (whose narratives I will shortly analyse in detail) complain bitterly about their lot. They show no patience or acceptance of the miseries inherent in mortal life and end up expressing a death-wish that bears no relation to the godly and lawful desire of death permitted by all churchmen whose teachings Spenser would have heard or read and, in the fiction of *The Faerie Queene*, by Contemplation. Where good Christians, having completed their earthly tasks, express a holy yearning to see "God face to face"

(Becon, *Sicke Mannes Salue* 178),[44] Spenser's despairing characters, unwilling to go on toiling and suffering, are tempted to abandon their quest and life in the "middest of the race" (*FQ* 1.7.5).

It is notable that the stories of the Spenserian death-wishers are told in a very sympathetic tone; the text is often pervaded by a sense of melancholic understanding for human vulnerability in the face of the hardships of life. The sorrows of the human condition are certainly not minimized in Spenser's work. On the contrary, life is represented as burdened with toil and pain, and all sorts of characters, the virtuous and the wicked, the brave and the fearful, are likely to fall prey, at some point in their life, to exhaustion. Many of Spenser's characters express more or less vehemently the sense that all their labouring yields only ephemeral hence vain fruits, while frustration and suffering are unavoidable companions. The voice of Spenser's narrator, in fact, becomes more lyric, passionate and unconventional when it describes people's unwillingness or perhaps incapacity to accept their own condition as mortals in a fallen world and conform to the contemporary ideals of Christian patience and Stoic endurance.

Yet, if Spenser's work encourages sympathy for human frailty and an understanding of the fact that, as mortals, people are necessarily subject to passions and desires that expose them to temptation, frustration and loss, the misunderstanding, manifested by some characters, of the godly significance of life and death, is not condoned. The context of Spenser's narratives always makes it clear that they function as warnings or didactic devices, part of a rhetorical strategy to make the Christian significance of life and death emerge. Thus when an unorthodox desire for death is expressed not, as I shall discuss below, by evil characters, but by Redcrosse or Una, Spenser emphasizes that

---

[44] The orthodox death-wish quoted is uttered by the dying Epaphroditus. All *artes moriendi* present versions of the exemplary godly desire of death on which good Christians should model their own and whose patterns are found in the Scriptures; see for instance David's address to God in Psalm 42: "My soule thirsteth for God, for the liuing God, when shall I come and appeare before God?"

they are manifestly deluded or momentarily maddened by grief. Their disheartenment, I suggest, is dramatized in order to stimulate reflections on mortal weakness, not for imitation.

4. Christian Death-Wish and Weariness of Life

There are very few instances in Spenser's work of a desire of death linked explicitly and directly to a desire for eternity, and the few there are seem to me highly ambiguous. The emphasis in Spenser's narratives lies rather on yearning for death seen as a very secular and merely human aspiration that does not conform to the pattern of the Christian godly desire of death as established by contemporary theology and illustrated in Book 1, canto 10 of *The Faerie Queene*. I suggest that even the death-wish Redcrosse expresses in the House of Holiness may be classified among those seemingly pious but really "condemnable death wishes" which were the object of theological reprimand (Abbot 260).

More intensely and more often than any other character in Spenser, Redcrosse manifests an inclination to despair and a yearning for death. This is not surprising given that his narratives dramatize the way to holiness within which, in Protestant terms, the experience of despair (in its godly and ungodly aspects) is climactic. As I will demonstrate, the loss of will to live that Redcrosse manifests in the House of Holiness and elsewhere arises more from his lack of spiritual joy and his mortal view of life's toils and sorrows than from a "fervent desire [. . .] to be with the blessed Trinity and the angels about the throne" (Abbot 259).

Significantly epitomized as "the man that would not liue" (1.10.27), Redcrosse is beyond doubt the most representative death-wisher in *The Faerie Queene*. Since he is introduced as a type of the melancholy man, "his cheere did seeme too solemne sad" (1.1.2), any Elizabethan reader instructed in the symptoms and manifestations of *the* malady thanks to the abundant and widespread literature on the subject would have expected him to be predisposed to bitter meditation on life and intense yearning for death.[45] His sad "cheere" would also have sug-

---

[45] In Spenser's day, it was universally held that melancholy stimulates *taedium vitae*. Babb and Lyons trace sixteenth-century commonplaces and popular beliefs as regards the malady and its presumed symptoms. The fact that some

II The Psychology of Despair

gested sadness as lack of that joy that is a "frute of the Spirit" (Gal. 5.22) from which "followes peace of conscience, and from peace comes joy in the holy Ghost" (Perkins, *Whole Treatise* 35).

The Spenserian death-wisher par excellence, Redcrosse appropriately leads the procession of those who, unwilling to bear tribulations, and unaware of their providential purpose, make death the object of their yearning, expecting from it the simultaneous end of their existence and the annihilation of their sufferings. Upon hearing a voice through the door while he is trapped in Orgoglio's dungeon, Redcrosse introduces himself to the stranger as one belonging in the number of those who "liue in liues despight" (2.1.36): in fact he declares he has to "liue perforce" (1.8.38). This vision of people who live unwillingly, who feel life is so painful to them that they see it as a kind of protracted agony never relieved by death, or else a never-ending death bringing no rest but only hellish torments, is one of the crucial and recurrent themes in Spenser's work. While Spenser's emphasis on this theme is no doubt part of the strategy he employs to illustrate fleshly views of life and death in which hatred of life signals not a godly detachment from earthly things, but a loathing of them arising from a failure of nerve in the face of tribulations, nevertheless it receives remarkable and sympathetic treatment.

The Faerie Queene often represents this hatred of life through the motif of a living death. Redcrosse refers to himself as one who lies "dying euery stound" (1.8.38), waiting anxiously for physical death to put an end to the kind of living death, or hell on earth, he is experiencing. Not surprisingly he hopes the person calling through the door in Orgoglio's dungeon is his executioner, one who will offer him "happy choyce / Of death" (st. 38). His present situation is so distressing and the "balefull darkenesse" of his physical prison which emblematizes his moral state seems so dense, that he greets the stranger he takes for

---

of the cures Redcrosse receives in the House of Holiness were those administered to the melancholy (see Babb 51-52 and 72) confirms his presentation as that of a melancholic.

his murderer with words full of hope and expectation: "O welcome thou, that doest of death bring tydings trew" (st. 38).

Once out of the dungeon thanks to Arthur's intervention, Redcrosse's mood remains unchanged, despite Arthur's and Una's display of affection and efforts at reviving love of life and duty in him; immediately after he is rescued, in fact, his death-wish becomes a suicidal urge. Despair, "a man of hell" (1.9.28), has only to represent to him life as an occasion for sin and suffering to persuade the melancholy, conscience-burdened knight that death is a boon to be actively sought. Redcrosse who, as Despair reminds him, "for death so oft did call" when shut up in Orgoglio's dungeon, is now fully convinced he has "greatest need" of death (1.9.45). Life, far from being the Christian paradigm apparently promised through the narrative of Book 1, a progress towards Holiness through trials and setbacks, now appears as a retrogressive immersion into evil, sin and sorrow. It is not a process towards a goal, but a degeneration that Redcrosse wants to interrupt as soon as possible by choosing death. Since Spenser's well-schooled Christian reader knows that wrong premises necessarily produce wrong conclusions, he or she understands that Redcrosse's attitude to life and death, arising from the unorthodox views he holds while he is beside himself with despair, is not proposed as a model. It is clear that Redcrosse's loathing of life and longing for death has not much in common with the godly detachment from earthly things and victory over fear of death on which all *artes moriendi* focus.

Few incidents in the *Faerie Queene* are as predictable as Redcrosse's encounter with Despair in Book 1, canto 9.[46] In fact, within the framework of Redcrosse's narratives (the "Legende [. . .] of Holinesse"), the episode is a thematically inescapable incident. Spenser had to reduce the gap between his everyman's final condition as the champion of holiness, and his state after no less than two thirds of the book as a joyless Christian inclining to put faith in the wrong objects

---

[46] A version of my discussion of Redcrosse's suicidal temptation was published in *Cahiers Elisabéthains*.

and rely on his human resources. "The beginning of the fall of man was trust in himselfe. The beginning of the restoring of man, was distrust in himselfe, and trust in God": thus Elizabeth's *Prayer Book* concisely described the precondition of regeneration (Snyder 29). In order to become the pattern of the Protestant saint Redcrosse must despair of himself and put all his trust in God. This he can do only by replacing his proud self-assurance with awareness of his "frail nature," "wicked will," and "sinful life" (Becon, *Sicke Mannes Salue* 107), and of his condition as "a sinner, guilty of everlasting damnation" and incapable of fulfilling God's law through his own "works and perfection" (Becon, *Dialogue* 629). He must, in fact, undergo that experience of despair whose centrality in the sixteenth-century Protestant ideology is attested by the space devoted to it in the works of theologians, natural and moral philosophers, men of letters, and authors of autobiographies.[47]

Despair was not the invention of Protestantism; however, by assigning it a central place in its theology of salvation Protestantism certainly laid unprecedented stress on it and deepened its inherent contradictions. From the time of the Pauline discussion of the saving nature of "godly sorow" (2 Cor. 7.10) that arises from acknowledgement of sins and stimulates repentance, the idea of the fruitfulness of *tristitia* had implanted itself in the Christian psyche. So had the awareness of the spiritual danger inherent in "worldly sorow [which] causeth death" (2 Cor. 7.10). Indeed, a survey of the writings of the most influential

---

[47] A look at the *General Index to the Publications of the Parker Society* under the heading "despair" (but see also "affliction," "temptation," and "tribulation") gives an idea of the theological concern. Anyone familiar with sixteenth-century medical tracts knows how fully the effects of despair are dealt with in such writings. As for literary treatments of despair, suffice it to note the motif's centrality in morality plays (still popular in the Renaissance), and its dramatization on the Elizabethan and Jacobean stage (see Wymer). An illuminating example in personal writings is *The Autobiography of Thomas Whythorne*. Whythorne (1528-1596), a musician, is the author of one of the earliest English autobiographies.

theologians from Augustine (fourth-fifth centuries) to Bonaventura (thirteenth century) shows that for centuries the emphasis had fallen more on the threat to the mental and spiritual welfare of Christians of excessive sorrow for sin and loathing of self, than on the saving potential of godly *tristitia*.[48] Things changed with the advent of Protestantism with its view of Grace as a gratuitous gift that the elect receive when they make themselves apt recipients of it through acknowledgement of their helplessness, sinfulness, and worthlessness. Hence the necessity of the experience of despair that accompanies the realization of the corruption and insufficiency of human attempts to gain forgiveness for sins and salvation.[49]

Neither Calvin nor the Anglican theologians, however, subscribed to Luther's exhortations to Christians to venture "even to the abyss of despair."[50] While they allowed that the experience of despair is a prerequisite to conversion, they warned that venturing as far as the "abyss of despair" entails fatal risks, as one may not come out again. Echoing Aquinas's warning against allowing "fear of God or horror of one's own sins [. . .] to be an occasion to despair" (2: 475) and reminding his readers that "the Apostle (2 Cor. 2.7) did not wish those who repented to be swallowed up with overmuch sorrow," Calvin attempts to bal-

---

[48] I follow Snyder who provides such a survey and discusses the texts that develop the medieval view of despair as "an excess or perversion of a wholesome emotion" (35).

[49] In this sense, Donald A. Beecher rightly argues that within the Protestant view "the psychology of despair becomes an integral part of the doctrine of redemption"; it is a crisis that "propels man back to God" ("Anatomy" 97). It is common knowledge that unlike the Protestants, Roman Catholics attach great importance to good works and believe that to a certain extent their efforts can win them salvation. For a scholarly discussion of the Catholic theology of salvation, see Swanson, *Religion and Devotion in Europe, c. 1215-c. 1515*, esp. Chapter 2.

[50] In the same passage Luther eulogizes the experience of despair as "beautiful" and "near to Grace" (qtd. in Snyder 59). Snyder cites other relevant passages from Luther's writings about despair and indicates modern critical editions of his work.

ance reminders of irremediable human perversity and corruption with urgings not to give way to despair:

> But after man's rebellion, our eyes – wherever they turn – encounter God's curse. This curse, while it seizes and envelops innocent creatures through our fault, must overwhelm our souls with despair. [. . .] Yet we must remember to exercise restraint, lest sorrow engulf us. For nothing more readily happens to fearful consciences than falling into despair. And also by this stratagem, whomever Satan sees overwhelmed by the fear of God he more and more submerges in that deep whirlpool of sorrow that they may never rise again. (1: 341, 609)

The difference between "godly sorrow" and "damnable despair" (Perkins, *Whole Treatise* 2: 24), or to put it another way, the paradoxical nature of despair as a door opening either onto salvation or damnation is an often treated subject in Elizabethan devotional writings. The etymology itself signals the deadly potential of despair: the word "derives from the privative of 'to hope' (Lat. *espere*); theologically, deprivation of hope denies the possibility of salvation since the fundamental condition of transcendent grace is faith in its possibility" (Dixon 39). Richard McCabe puts it with a felicitous succinctness: "the psychological trick was to despair of all but grace," but "the moral danger was despair of grace itself" (*Pillars* 67). To judge from the words of influential divines like Thomas Becon, the "trick" was not easily performed even by scrupulous churchmen:

> I have in times past heard by the relation of certain credible persons, how greatly divers godly and virtuous men have been troubled in their consciences by the consideration of their former life, which hath appeared to them so horrible and sinful, that they have not only cursed the day of their birth, as we read of Job and Jeremy, but also been at the point of falling into desperation [. . .]. And I myself before few years did

know certain men of an honest conversation and approved judgement (of whom some be yet living, worthy and valiant champions in the court of the Most Highest), which were so turmoiled and tossed with the raging and cruel waves of desperation, that scarcely there remained any hope of salvation in their breasts; so terrible and loathsome appeared the face of their life to the eyes of their mind. (Becon, *Dialogue* 622)

Concern about the frequency with which the experience of despair might go beyond a saving grief for sins and get dangerously near a damning despair of divine mercy, is a leitmotiv in the writings of the most influential theologians. This preoccupation may register a consequence of the Protestant emphasis on self-examination. As Donald Beecher notes, "given the intense examination of the soul that arose with the Lutheran principle of the priesthood of every believer and the Calvinist doctrine of election, the threat of despair became an integral part of the Reformation psyche" ("Anatomy" 86). It is not hard to imagine how constant reflections on human postlapsarian corruption, exhausting examinations of conscience and painful searches of signs of the working of Grace could lead some people to feel "surcharged with the bondage and horror of their sinnes, [their] distressed conscience" oppressed with "conceit of unpardonablenesse" of their sins (Sym 248) and awareness that nobody can "say with a safe conscience and undoubted faith, I am of the number of God's elect" (Becon, *Sicke Mannes Salue* 174).[51] By general consent, there were two potential outcomes to crises of this kind: conversion or surrender to fatal de-

---

[51] Protestants could not count on the balm for burdened consciences available to Roman Catholics in the form of confession and indulgences. Rejection of the idea of Purgatory and of the efficacy of prayers for the dead had heightened anxiety about one's election as no further chance of salvation was possible in the afterlife. The relation between this anxiety and despair was well established: McCabe points out that "the seventeenth article of the Established Church, 'De Praedestinatione et Electione', concludes its doctrinal formulations with a warning against desperation" (*Pillars* 158).

spair often followed by suicide. William Perkins juxtaposes the diverging roads of those who following their descent to the "pit of despaire" recover faith in God's grace and mercy, and of those who do not:

> For even of those that feare God, and have received to beleeve, there be many, who in the time of their distresses, when they have considered the weight and desert of their sinnes, and withall apprehended the wrath of God due unto them, have been brought unto hard exigents, mourning and wailing, and crying out, as if God had forsaken them, untill they have beene releeved by the Spirit of Christ [. . .]. [Others] despairing of the mercy of God, and their own salvation, [. . .] have either growne to phrensie and madnesse, or else sorted unto themselves fearefull ends, some by hanging, some by drowning, others by embruing their hands in their owne bloud. (Perkins, *Whole Treatise*, "Epistle Dedicatory")

Medical writers agreed with theologians that the "goodmans conscience" was often the field where battles that caused "extreme miserie" were fought, and they, too, warned that "religious melancholy" could arouse suicidal urges (Wright 230).[52] The causal relationship between religious despair and suicide was also a well-established literary topos and a recurrent theme in the personal writings of Christians who described the crises preceding their conversion.[53]

---

[52] On sixteenth-century discussions of religious melancholy and its inherent risks, see Babb 47-54. The expression "religious melancholy" is in the title of sect. 4, member 1, subsect. 1 of Robert Burton's *The Anatomy of Melancholy* (1621); of particular interest with respect to my discussion of Redcrosse's narrative is subsection 3 which deals with "Causes of Despaire, the Divell, Melancholy, Meditation, Distrust, Weaknesse of Faith, Rigid Ministers, Misunderstanding Scriptures, Guilty Consciences, etc." (3: 411).

[53] On literary dramatizations of the relation between despair and suicide, see Rolfs and Wymer. See also the *Variorum* edition of Spenser's work which

That the climactic experience in the Protestant progress to holiness could be the door onto damnation for those whose lack of saving faith had led them to become murderers of themselves, endowed the topic of despair with a paradoxical quality whose ethic, didactic, and aesthetic potential Spenser exploits artfully as I will show in the following pages. By linking, through the narratives of his everyman and saint-to-be, the themes of despair with those of holiness and suicide, Spenser dramatizes the dangers and rewards inherent in the Christian experience. His narrative of Redcrosse's temptation to suicide illustrates a lesson that in his days a large number of moral plays, deathbed manuals, and treatments of the consequences of religious despair in medical tracts dealt with, viz, that "the child of God may passe to heaven by the very gulfes of hell" (Perkins, *Salve* 492). What makes Spenser's own dramatization of this worn discourse distinctive is his dramatic mastery in creating a sense of the uncertainty of the outcome of Redcrosse's duel with Despair. What is also remarkable is the evocative quality of his representations of Redcrosse's suffering while he traverses the "gulph of desperation" (Perkins, *Salve* 492) and of the dreariness of the world seen through the lens of despair, that is, wanting God's love.

Both from a narrative and a thematic point of view Redcrosse's encounter with Despair is a carefully prepared incident, the climax of a process whose double encoding reflects the double nature of despair. In the course of the first eight cantos of Book 1 the inexperienced knight, characterized by pride, rashness, and self-reliance, abandons Una because of her presumed unfaithfulness, kills Sansfoy and sports his shield, champions and loves Duessa, fights with Sansjoy in the

---

indicates the narrative of Cordelia's suicidal despair in the *Mirrour of Magistrates* (1: 270-72). MacDonald and Murphy discuss some interesting writings by early seventeenth-century individuals and argue that the Puritans "institutionalized suicidal moods, presenting them as the emotional symbol of the liminal stage between the sinful life and regeneration. For this reason some converts may actually have exaggerated their torment in their autobiographies" (65).

House of Pride obtaining only a partial victory, and is finally captured by Orgoglio. Since Spenser himself indicates the allegorical significance of his characters (by for example giving them self-explanatory names as in the case of the Sans brothers, or Una and Duessa who in the argument to 1.2 are indicated as "Truth" and "falshood"), it is clear that Redcrosse represents a Christian knight who, albeit not willingly and knowingly, has abandoned truth, struggles with faithlessness (not lack of faith in God, but lack of faith in truth or the truth of the true church), puts faith in the wrong objects, lacks that joy that is a "frute of the Spirit" (Gal. 5.22), and is the prisoner of his fleshly self. In the light of Elizabethan religious discourses, these episodes can be read at the same time as Redcrosse's progressive immersion into sinfulness and worldly sorrow which could lead him to fatal despair and suicide, or as stages towards his gaining awareness of his human corruption and insufficiency, a condition characterized by godly sorrow which could lead him to salvation if he invokes divine mercy. What from one point of view is Redcrosse's steady movement away from truth and into error, from another point of view can be seen as a steady movement towards the crisis that brings about his conversion.

Redcrosse's encounter with Despair is preceded and prepared by his first experience of despair when he meets Orgoglio, an incident that also allows two seemingly contradictory readings. One is obvious given Spenser's association of Orgoglio with an earthquake, a Scriptural "omen of the Last Judgement" (Hamilton 93, 2001 ed. of *FQ*): in this reading, the sinful and slothful Redcrosse becomes the object of God's wrath and receives due punishment. Imprisoned in his fleshly pride and lacking faith in salvation (when he is surprised by Orgoglio the knight has divested himself of the armour of Christ and wears no "helmet of salvation," Eph. 6.16), Redcrosse is incapable of calling to God for help, is overwhelmed by worldly sorrow, and invokes death

(1.8.38).[54] He is saved from damning despair by divine Grace, whose agent is Arthur. From another perspective, however, the same incident is a necessary and fruitful experience, a crucial step forward on the way to conversion. Redcrosse cannot become the pattern of the new Christian knight and Protestant saint unless his fleshly lusts and trusts are mortified, unless, that is, his old self dies.

The knight whom Orgoglio attacks is remarkably self-satisfied; proud of his chivalric exploits that have proved his martial prowess, convinced of having preserved his honour by forsaking his unfaithful lady and of having fulfilled his duties as a courteous knight by championing the cause of the wronged Fidessa, he enjoys the pleasures offered by a welcoming and amorous partner (1.7.2-3 and 7). The fact that he is portrayed by the narrator as one "carelesse of his health," of his moral and spiritual health, and of "his fame" (1.7.7) (a fame that depends on completion of his quest whose spiritual significance is clear), signals that his expectations and perspectives are fleshly and earthly. He has reached that height of the experience of pride in self necessary to realize one's helplessness. "Disarmed all of yron-coted Plate" (1.7.2), he must gain awareness of the ugliness of his "clownish," viz, fleshly self (*FQ*, "A Letter of the Authors").[55] In this perspective, his struggle with Orgoglio and his deep suffering in his dungeon are like labour pains that Redcrosse must endure to give birth to his new self. Spenser's choice of words at 1.8.40 to describe Arthur's effort to deliver Redcrosse from the dungeon/womb, "long paines" and "labours manifold," seems to confirm a deliberate allusion in this sense. Orgoglio's "Dongeon deepe" (1.7.15) functions as a sepulchre where Redcrosse's old self is buried and whence the resurrection of his new self starts. Its description as a "deepe descent, as

---

[54] For a selection of scholarly discussions of the allegorical significances of the Orgoglio episode, see the useful list of references appended to Hugh Maclean's article "Orgoglio."

[55] The "Letter" describes the clownish aspect of Redcrosse before he wears the armour of Christ.

II The Psychology of Despair 47

darke as hell, / That breathed euer forth a filthie banefull smell" (1.8.39) may be read as yet another allusion to the dual nature of despair as spiritual death and door onto salvation through intense suffering in confirmation of the view that whom God "will lift up into heaven, him he bringeth down first unto hell" (Becon, *Solace* 577).

Upon his emergence from Orgoglio's dungeon, Redcrosse is described as a "ruefull spectacle of death and ghastly drere," "his sad dull eyes deepe sunck in hollow pits," "his visage pale and wan," "his vitall powres / Decayd, and all his flesh shronk vp like withered flowres" (1.8.40-42). Redcrosse's corpse-like aspect has, I believe, three main encodings: one is as a conventional description of the outward signs of melancholy (whether erotic or religious) that was found in every popular tract of natural philosophy of the day and that had become a literary and dramatic cliché.[56] A second encoding is Scriptural representations of the aspect of prophets such as Jonah, Job, or David who had suffered temptation or who had been conscience-burdened and whose stories were favourites with preachers of the period. Thus William Perkins observes that the "Distress arising of a divine temptation [. . .] workes a change and alteration in the body, as it were a burning ague [. . .] and consumes the flesh more than any sicknesse can do"; as proof of the truth of his words he calls "the word of God" and David's own testimony to witness: "*David* in this distresse affirmeth, *that his eyes were eaten as it were with worms, and sunck into his head*, Psa. 6.7" (*Whole Treatise* 27). Finally, those descriptions of Redcrosse after he leaves his cell which emphasize the motif of death develop the theme of the death of Redcrosse's "old self." Redcrosse's physical decay may be a sign of the growing weakness of the "old man" in him, signifying that the mortal part of him, his "body of sinne" (Rom. 6.6), is being consumed.

Albeit in agony, the "old man" in Redcrosse is not dead yet and Una's remark that her knight is "weake and wearie" (1.9.20) may be

---

[56] Well-documented discussions of Renaissance medical descriptions and literary representations of melancholy people are found in Babb and Lyons.

seen either as a confirmation of this or as a signal that Redcrosse's freedom after he has left the dungeon is merely physical, because his spirit is still prisoner to despair.[57] Whether the "new man" in Redcrosse still struggles for life with the dying "old man" or Redcrosse's body is free while his spirit is still imprisoned in sorrow because he has learned not to rely on his human resources but has not learned yet to abandon himself to God's mercy, the reader who learns from the argument to canto 9 that Redcrosse is about to meet "Despayre" has reason to think that the struggle will be very hard. Thus Spenser encourages readers' sympathy for his unprepared and frail everyman.

The incident of Redcrosse's encounter with Trevisan (1.9.21-32) that on the narrative level serves as a prelude to the climactic encounter of the Despair Canto, on the thematic level serves to develop the motif of Redcrosse's unpreparedness to fight a victorious spiritual fight. A "weake and wearie" Redcrosse who travels with a worried Una aware that she must slow "her forward course" since her "chosen knight" is in no state to fight the final fight against the dragon (1.9.20), comes across a knight on the run. The stranger looks terrified and in a state of confusion. No "drop of bloud in all his face appears / Nor life in limbe" (1.9.22); he is "sencelesse and aghast" (st. 23), "staring wide / With stony eyes, and hartlesse hollow hew, / Astonisht stood, as one that had aspide / Infernall furies, with their chaines vntide" (st. 24). Redcrosse seems not to notice the striking resemblance between himself at the moment he emerged from Orgoglio's dungeon and the unfortunate stranger. In fact he affirms: "neuer knight I saw in such misseeming plight" (st. 23); by employing the same adjective used at 1.8.42, where Una describes Redcrosse's "hew" as "misseeming," Spenser obtains an effect of irony that further emphasizes the "blindness" of Redcrosse that his failure to recognize himself in Fradubio or the Sans brothers had already signalled. As A. C. Hamilton notes, the stranger whose "head" is "vnarmd" (st. 22) "appears as

---

[57] Redcrosse's weakness and weariness, in fact, are clearly not physical, but moral since he has had food and rest in 1.8.50.

did the Red Cross Knight before his fall, 'Disarmd, disgrast, and inwardly dismayde'" (1977 ed. of *FQ* 123). Given the Pauline association of the helmet with the "hope of saluation" (1 Thess. 5.8), reference to Trevisan's unarmed head is clearly meant to signal the theme of despair as lack of saving hope. Another detail of Trevisan's description, the "hempen rope he weares" around his neck (st. 22), links this projection of Redcrosse with the temptation to suicide that Spenser's contemporaries saw as the issue of fatal despair.[58]

Even though in the eyes of Spenser's careful readers Trevisan's bare head and the halter around his neck would have been clear enough evidence of the fact that he had experienced despair, the knight openly describes himself as a victim of "that cursed wight," "a man of hell, that cals himselfe Despaire" (1.9.28). Trevisan explains how Despair exploited his own and his friend's wordly dissatisfactions to lead them to final desperation: having noticed that they were unhappy lovers, Despair first deprived them of hope, then offered a knife to Terwin who accepted it and killed himself, and a halter to Trevisan, who fled. This is another element (beside the reiterated use of the word "misseeming" as noted above) that suggests an identification of Trevisan with Redcrosse whose long and gradual journey towards final despair begins in Book 1, canto 2, when, deceived by Archimago into believing in Una's unfaithfulness, he finds himself "in torment great, / And bitter anguish" (st. 6). On the narrative level the onset of his moral and spiritual confusion coincides with his becoming an unhappy lover; from then on, "will was his guide, and griefe led him astray" (1.2.12). Hence encoded in Trevisan's distraught state, a consequence of his condition as a love-melancholic, is the discourse, dramatized by Redcrosse's narratives (and many others in the poem, notably that of the suicide Amavia at 2.1), that unchecked passions endanger people's

---

[58] Snyder argues that the scriptural portrayal of the suicide Judas hanging from a tree initiated the tradition of iconographic representations of despair as a figure hanging itself, as in Giotto's despair fresco at Padua, one of the masterpieces Snyder mentions (55-56).

balance. Another encoding is the common view, which theologians and physicians stressed with equal vehemence, of melancholy as the "Devils bait" or "Balneum Diaboli," an idea that arises from the conviction that "the Devill being well acquainted with the complexion and temperature of man [. . .] conveys himselfe into this humor" to drive people to despair.[59] Of all types of melancholy, love or erotic melancholy was the most familiar to readers of poetry and theatre goers, and that more frequently discussed in tracts of natural philosophy. This fact may have influenced Spenser's choice to make Trevisan and Terwin love-melancholics, a choice that may also signal his desire to arouse sympathy for his characters at the same time as the narrative censures their attitudes.[60]

As well as functioning as an example of worldly sorrow and as a possible projection of Redcrosse's psychic state, Trevisan also serves to further the pathos of Spenser's narrative of Redcrosse's struggle with Despair and to widen its didactic aims. Trevisan's encounter with Redcrosse, in fact, develops the motif of the knight's unpreparedness and introduces the motif of grace that will be climactic in the narrative of Redcrosse's rescue from suicidal impulses.

---

[59] The first and third quotations are from Perkins, *Whole Treatise* 46; the second is from Burton, sect. 4, member 1, subsect. 1, 3: 411. Cf. Hamlet's fear that the spirit he has seen "May be the devil, and the devil hath power / T'assume a pleasing shape; yea, and perhaps, / Out of my weakness and my melancholy – / As he is very potent with such spirits – / Abuses me to damn me" (2.2.601-605).

[60] It is not surprising that the theme of erotic melancholy appears in a canto whose subject is religious despair; the two issues were commonly associated in Spenser's day as two forms of love melancholy, distinguished in object (a person and God respectively), but characterized by the same symptoms and consequences. Beecher argues that to Tudor eyes "they are in essence one and the same phenomenon, differing in few respects in the way they transfix the soul and thereby generate that deteriorating complicity of depraved judgement and adust humours that leads, in turn, to common ends: moroseness, despair and suicide" ("Anatomy " 85).

Although Redcrosse had invoked death in Orgoglio's dungeon as a deliverance from his present evils, his death-wish had been "passive" as he had expressed an intense desire to die, but no intent to kill himself. Now, listening to Trevisan's account, he is confronted with an "active" death-wish, a suicidal urge. His initial attitude to Trevisan is one of superficial censure and incredulity when he wonders how the temptation to self-destruction can possibly overcome the natural instinct of self-preservation: "How may a man (said he) with idle speech / Be wonne, to spoyle the Castle of his health?" (1.9.31). The fact that he calls Despair's persuasive words (reported to him by Trevisan in st. 29) "idle speech" alerts the reader, well-warned in moral plays and deathbed manuals of the rhetorical skills of the evil spirits or the devil, to Redcrosse's unpreparedness for Despair's verbal attack and his own human frailty.[61] Trevisan, "whom triall late did teach" (1.9.31) how thoughts engendered by despair progressively invade the soul, tries to open Redcrosse's eyes:

> His subtill tongue, like dropping honny, mealt'th
> Into the hart, and searcheth euery vaine,
> That ere one be aware, by secret stealth
> His powre is reft, and weaknesse doth remaine. (1.9.31)

Trevisan's description of the paralyzing effect of Despair's words on the reason and will closes with a vehement exhortation to Redcrosse: "O neuer Sir desire to try his guilefull traine" (1.9.31). The verb "desire" is significant, since it signals the motif of Redcrosse's rashness and trust in self that make him eager to display his superior judgement and resistance. In fact, to Trevisan's entreaty Redcrosse replies that he will "neuer rest, / Till I that treachours art haue heard and tride" (st. 32). In the light of Trevisan's warning that "like infirmitie like chaunce may heare" (st. 30), Redcrosse's impatience to face Despair in the conviction that he can do better than the two knights indi-

---

[61] Latimer warns that the devil is "an old doctor, and very well learned in the Scripture" (2: 149).

cates that he does not recognize his share in human "infirmitie." The motif of his excessive self-confidence is further emphasized by his protectiveness towards Trevisan whom he "comforted in feare" (st. 34) when they approach Despair's cave.

Stanza 37 is central for Spenser's construction of pathos for Redcrosse's imminent struggle with Despair in that it epitomizes and amplifies the motif of the knight's fleshly assurance that seems to portend a debacle. Confronted by the "piteous spectacle" (1.9.37) of the suicide Terwin, "all wallowd in his owne yet luke-warme blood" (st. 36), Redcrosse "with firie zeale [. . .] burnt in courage bold, / Him to auenge, before his bloud were cold" (st. 37). What is activated is his warriour courage, the "zeale" that had animated him in his early fights fought in compliance with the dictates of the honour-shame paradigm and to prove his martial prowess. Reference to his intention to "auenge" Terwin's death signals on the one hand an assumption on the part of Redcrosse of the role of avenger on no official authority and upon his own judgement. On the other, his vows of revenge and the assertion that Despair should pay with his blood for Terwin's death, reveal that he puts himself under the Law of the Old Testament, not of the Gospel, and since according to the Law all deserve damnation because nobody can fulfil the precepts set by it, this perspective predisposes Redcrosse to fall into despair. He ignores that "Christ is the fulfilling of the law for every one that believeth unto righteousness" (Becon, *Dialogue* 629).[62]

Redcrosse's response to the sight of the dead Terwin is dramatized as mistaken; this sight should have reminded Redcrosse of the fate awaiting the victims of despair and should have stimulated reflections on his own frailty, leading him to cry to God for help against the temp-

---

[62] Redcrosse's promise that Despair must with his own "bloud [. . .] price his [Terwin's] bloud" anticipates Despair's statement that "life must life, and bloud must bloud repay" (1.9.43). Kathleen Williams rightly claims that "Red Crosse is moving towards the sorrow and fear of the law of guilt and vengeance, away from the true faith of salvation in Christ" (16).

tation to despair. Instead, it stimulates his fleshly pride. In lieu of acknowledging his own insufficiency, once again in his pride he thinks he does not need God's assistance in his spiritual warfare and trusts he can confront and defeat Despair by himself. As the narrator comments at 1.10.1, whoever counts on "fleshly might, / And vaine assurance of mortality, / [. . .] / Against spirituall foes, yeelds by and by." Redcrosse, in fact, seems destined to a fatal defeat.

The multiple references in Trevisan's speech to the unexpected working of Grace, point to the possibility that the dénouement could be otherwise. Trevisan's mention of divine love, "Gods deare loue," and help, "God from him me blesse" (1.9.25, 28), evoke God's mercy which is the heart of Una's appeal to Redcrosse at 1.9.53 when, having prevented his suicide, she urges him to trust in "heauenly mercies." When Trevisan acknowledges that he would have killed himself "had not greater grace / Me *reft* from him [Despair]" (st. 26; emphasis mine), I think the physicality expressed by the verb *to reave* ('to take away by force') deliberately parallels and anticipates Una/Grace's act of snatching the knife from Redcrosse's suicidal hand (1.9.52). In both cases the text develops the view of the irresistible force of Grace and of the power of despair whose victims must be reft from its deadly embrace.

The lively and significant dialogue between Trevisan and Redcrosse prepares for the climax of the canto, Redcrosse's encounter with Despair, an incident whose narrative structure, vocabulary, and rhetorical patterning are highly conventional.[63] Spenser's art succeeds in infusing these trite commonplaces with pathos and in distinguishing Redcrosse's narrative from the countless almost identical treatments of fights with despair in devotional and literary works. It does so espe-

---

[63] Beecher rightly argues that "the question of specific sources for Spenser is quite irrelevant since the motif had become commonplace; any representation would have served as well as another" ("Spenser's Redcrosse Knight" 4). Beecher however does meticulously trace the literary sources of the Despair canto both in the above article and in his "Anatomy."

cially, as we shall see, through a careful emphasis on Redcrosse's physical and moral suffering, and through an artful exploitation of the dual nature of despair which allows two opposite outcomes of Redcrosse's crisis, one fatal, the other blessed.

Contemporary readers were familiar with the narrative and rhetorical patterns Spenser adopts for the Despair Canto, which are mainly those of medieval morality plays and sixteenth-century psychomachies, described so often in religious tracts. From popular morality plays such as *Mankind* or Skelton's *Magnyfycence* Spenser borrows the conventional dramatic sequence of sin, despair, salvation. In both plays a figure representing mankind is offered a rope by Mischief and is saved at the very last moment by Grace personified: Mercy in *Mankind* and Good Hope in *Magnyfycence*. From contemporary religious literature the poet adopts the pattern of the struggle between God and Satan taking place in the soul of Christians and gets inspiration from countless descriptions of how the devil tempts man to self-murdering despair. The dialectic duel between Redcrosse and Despair is reminiscent of works like Thomas Becon's *The Dialogue between the Christian Knight and Satan*; the vocabulary of Despair and Redcrosse's arguments is very close to that employed especially in "deathbed literature," a genre well represented by Becon's popular *Sicke Mannes Salue*.[64] All these works drew extensively from the Scriptures, from the classics, from medieval writers and from the abundant Catholic and Protestant literature about guilt, sin and salvation.

Given the enormous popularity of the theme of the fight against despair and of works dramatizing it, Spenser is likely to have taken into consideration the expectations that the relevant theological, medical, and literary discourses of the day would have created in readers. Redcrosse's answers to Despair can be set against those given by pattern Christians (figures like Thomas Becon's Christian Knight), thus build-

---

[64] See Nancy Lee Beaty's *The Craft of Dying* and Ralph Houlbrooke's suggestive "The Puritan Death-bed, c. 1560 – c. 1660."

II The Psychology of Despair 55

ing expectations about the outcome of his fight. A sign of Spenser's deliberate positioning of himself within conventional discourses of despair is his borrowing of the setting for his narrative from literary and iconographic clichés. The "hollow caue," the "ghastly Owle," and the "old stockes and stubs of trees" (1.9.33, 34) compose a landscape that recalls those "anti-life, anti-health, anti-fertility images" used by the Early Fathers to dramatize the destructive potential of despair (Snyder 58).[65] Such images no doubt contributed to the codification of the iconographic representations of the connection between death and despair in medieval and Renaissance emblems, woodcuts, and paintings familiar to Spenser and his readers.[66] The presence by Despair's cave of corpses "scattered on the greene, / And throwne about the cliffs" (st. 34) of persons who had hanged themselves on the barren trees, signals that Spenser's text endorses the conventional association of despair with suicide.[67]

The context of Redcrosse's narrative which evokes the paradoxical significance death assumes within the Christian perspective adds further meaning to the conventional landscape of death. When Despair's

---

[65] Harold Skulsky interestingly argues that Despair's cave recalls one of the "*antra et cavernae* of the Augustinian memory [cf. *Confessions* 10.17], 'a something full of horror, O my God, a deep and boundless manifold; and this is the mind, and this is myself'" ("Spenser's Despair Episode" 228). The landscape around Despair is clearly a projection of Redcrosse's interior geography. Lyons points out that black bile or melancholy "produced dreams and visions connected with death and evil spirits, with night and with graveyards, and with the plants, animals or other objects that represented or embodied these" (44).

[66] Kathrine Koller argues that Spenser "is not describing a painting or emblem he has seen, he is composing a picture for us out of the common visual symbols of his time – a stock description" (135). At p. 135 she describes the landscape of death and despair painted by masters like Breughel and Bosch who use the same symbols as Spenser, viz, owls, gibbets, corpses, and stumps of trees.

[67] Snyder deals with the testimonies of this well-established association between despair and suicide in devotional writings and medieval iconography. On its literary dramatizations, see note 53 above.

cave is described as "Darke, dolefull, drearie, like a greedie graue, / That still for carrion carcases doth craue" (1.9.33), the reader may recall that Orgoglio's dungeon was equally likened to a grave (1.8.39) whence Redcrosse had emerged, thanks to Arthur/divine grace, as a death-like figure displaying the marks of what could either be the death pangs of the old man in him before spiritual rebirth, or the marks of a state of despair progressively leading him to spiritual death. Redcrosse is now about to enter another grave that could be the place of his spiritual death or a temporary dwelling prior to resurrection as a new man. Hence the signs of death visible on Redcrosse (Spenser gives the reader no reason to think that the knight's aspect has changed since his recent emergence from the dungeon), mirrored in Despair's own aspect, point to these two kinds of death.[68]

The studied parallelism between Redcrosse and Despair's features reinforced by repeated use of the same words with reference to both characters, authorizes interpretations of Despair as a projection of Redcrosse's psyche, of his burdened conscience and fear of God's wrath. Note how Despair's portrayal at 1.9.35 traces faithfully that of Redcrosse at 1.8.41:

Despair	Redcrosse
"Musing full *sadly*" (1.9.35)	"His *sad dull* eyes" (1.8.41)
"Lookt deadly *dull*" (st. 35)	
"his *hollow* eyne" (st. 35)	"*hollow* pits" (st. 41)
"*raw-bone* cheekes" (st. 35)	"*rawbone* armes" (st. 41)
"through penurie and pine" (st. 35)	"for want of better bits" (st. 41)
[his cheeks] "were *shronke* into his iawes" (st. 35; all italics mine)	"his flesh *shronk* vp" (st. 41)

---

[68] I am clearly not the first to notice the likeness between Redcrosse and Despair. However, to the best of my knowledge, other commentators do not do so in connection with the theme of the dual significance of death. Besides, unlike most critics, I am not content with indicating a general likeness; I argue instead for a studied parallelism between the portrayals of the two characters: see the following paragraph.

The seeming dialogue with the horrible creature may therefore be read as an internal debate, a spiritual fight similar to those described in both Catholic and Protestant *artes moriendi*.[69] In fact, Despair has a triple significance in that he represents the abstraction of despair, an objectification of Redcrosse's psychic state, and a figure of the devil.

The devil in person was often represented in the *artes moriendi* and in deathbed manuals in the act of trying to take the dying Christian's soul away from the good angel by persuading that person to final despair.[70] The devil, however, was thought to appear and speak to people not just at the point of their death: a Mr Lea, for example, told Richard Napier that "a malevolent spirit 'will speak often to him and appear in the likeness of a man [. . .] and would draw him away.'"[71] Natural philosophers like Thomas Wright linked physiological processes to spiritual temptation: Wright warned that the devil "by secret meanes can enter into the former parte of our braine, and there chop and chaunge our imaginations," and that by "stirring the humours" and "altering the blood" he can push Christians "to sinne" and make them "slouthfull in

---

[69] Thomas P. Roche Jr. points out that although the narrator leads readers to think that Una enters the cave with Redcrosse and perhaps Trevisan ("That darkesome caue *they* enter," 1.9.35; emphasis mine), she "resurfaces in the fiction only after Redcross is handed the dagger" (72); this has led a colleague of Roche, A. Walton Litz, to argue that the dialogue between Redcrosse and Despair is "taking place only in Redcrosse's mind. Only when he makes the physical action of grabbing the dagger does Una see what is happening" (72).

[70] One of Epaphroditus's neighbours in Becon's *Sicke Mannes Salue* refers to Satan's presence near the dying Christian's deathbed: "He [God] hath sent his holy angels hither unto you, even into this your chamber. [. . .] They have pitched their tents round about you, that they may keep you harmless and safe from the devouring teeth of Satan. They wait upon you diligently for your defence, and will never depart from you, till they receive your soul" (188).

[71] The Elizabethan mathematician John Dee wrote in his diary that three persons he knew committed suicide "by the fende his instigation" (MacDonald and Murphy 51). Richard Napier (1590-1634) was a prominent astrologer and medical practitioner.

the way of God" (294).[72] In their instructions to Christians on how to thwart the devil's attempts to drive them to suicidal despair, theologians often recapitulated the "scientific" and popular beliefs about apparitions, hallucinations, and inner voices. Thus John Sym illustrates the many ways suicidal urges arise in the mind:

> *First*, in some visible *apparition* of the *devill*, speaking to, and perswading a man to kill himselfe. *Which* hee doth *either outwardly* in some bodily shape, as he spake to *Eve*, and to our *Saviour Christ*: *or else inwardly* to the *fancie*, whereby a man thinks that he heares, or sees the *devill*, or some other, that can be none else but hee, bidding, or perswading him to *stab* himselfe, or to fling himselfe into the *water* ... *Secondly*, the devill doth powerfully move a man to kill himselfe, in manner *equivalent* to a commandment, by *internall suggestions*, and raising of such inward powerfull *motions* of self-killing in the minde, as can hardly be put out, or withstood.
>
> (246)

While they acknowledged the role of the devil in temptations to damnable despair, theologians also warned that his victims were nevertheless responsible for their fall, since their defeat in the spiritual fight signalled their faithlessness and lack of trust in God's mercy. As John Sym explains: "in *people* surcharged with the bondage and horror of their sinnes [. . .] the *devill* aggravates [. . .] the feare of the punishment due for them [and] obscures, or overshadowes the *grace* and *mercy* of God" (248). Hence by charging Despair with Terwin's suicide, by calling him "the author of this fact" (1.9.37), Redcrosse signals his lack of awareness of the human responsibility to withstand the temptation to despair by invoking divine help. It falls to a biassed speaker, Despair, to assert a view in line with the theological ortho-

---

[72] On melancholy hallucinations in the form of voices or visions of black men or devils, see some interesting quotations from popular Renaissance medical tracts in Babb 31, 42, and 46.

doxy of the day when he replies, "None else to death this man despayring driue, / But his owne guiltie mind" (1.9.38). This is clearly no promising start for Redcrosse's fight against the devil's *"internall suggestions"* (Sym 246), or "diuelish thoughts" as Una significantly describes them (st. 53), although at first he tries to resist (in a very unconvinced and ineffective way, as we shall see) by recalling to his mind the standard answers suggested by sermons and religious tracts to people struggling between despair and Christian hope.

Despair's first argument to convince Redcrosse to kill himself is reminiscent of the conception, dear to classical writers and philosophers and to many poets and thinkers after them, of death as a desirable end to human toil and suffering. The idea is introduced by Despair in a masterly way in these hypnotic verses: "Sleepe after toyle, port after stormie seas, / Ease after warre, death after life does greatly please" (1.9.40). I think the alliteration in 's' in the first line and the 's' sounds in the second, are meant to recall to the reader's mind words like 'eternal sleep' and 'silence,' words linked to a view of death as escape from life's toil. The image in Chaucer's *Pardoner's Tale*, familiar, of course, to Spenser, of the old and weary man knocking on the ground day and night to gain an entrance that is also an exit from life comes to mind and with it those disconsolate words calling death a grace: "But yet to me she wol nat do that grace, / For which ful pale and welkèd is my face" (199). In this light the dead Terwin is presented by Despair as enjoying "eternall rest / And happie ease" (1.9.40), a desirable state of perfect peace making even the instinctive fear of death disappear and the pains of violent death seem bearable and worth enduring.[73] Despair's words here are remarkably similar to Becon's:

What if some litle paine the passage haue,
That makes fraile flesh to feare the bitter waue? (1.9.40)

---

[73] The contrast of words with the grisly appearance of Terwin's body may suggest that this is not the kind of ease a Christian should long for.

> Who will not be content to suffer a little and short pain, that he may for ever after enjoy continual quietness and everlasting rest? (*Sicke Mannes Salue* 150)

The idea of death as a desirable end to pain and sorrow is tightly linked to a pessimistic view of life that Despair articulates through commonplaces:

> Feare, sicknesse, age, losse, labour, sorrow, strife,
> Paine, hunger, cold, that makes the hart to quake;
> And euer fickle fortune rageth rife,
> All which, and thousands mo do make a loathsome life.
>
> (1.9.44)[74]

The theme was developed by classical writers in both literary and philosophical works and was then exploited by Christian theologians and authors of popular devotional writings in order to distance people from this world. Death is desirable because it is the exit from a sinful and painful life on earth and the door opening on a state of perfect bliss in paradise, man's real homeland. Despair's depiction of death as good and life as loathsome echoes this motif of the *contemptus mundi*.[75]

---

[74] Cf. Despair's representation of life with Calvin's depiction of it in the *Institutes*:
> various deseases repeatedly trouble us: now plague rages; now we are cruelly beset by the calamities of war; now ice and hail, consuming the year's expectation, lead to barrenness, which reduces us to poverty; wife, parents, children, neighbors, are snatched away by death; our house is burned by fire. It is on account of these occurrences that men curse their life. (1: 701)

Medieval treatments of the *contemptus mundi* motif and sixteenth-century devotional writings abound in variations of Despair's pessimistic tirade.

[75] Koller remarks that Despair's arguments are reminiscent of those employed by classical philosophers like Cicero and Seneca, medieval moralists, and

II The Psychology of Despair   61

The first great temptation of Redcrosse is to crave the "ease" that is the leitmotif of Despair's first persuasive efforts in stanzas 38 and 40.[76] Despair represents stasis as a good because all that continues leads to evil; "rest" serves "Th'ill to preuent, that life ensewen may" (st. 44). As my discussion of Spenserian dramatizations of the death-wish motif shows (see Chapters 5 and 6 below), the temptation to escape the hardships of one's quest is a pervasive theme in *The Faerie Queene*, a longing that Spenser's narrator and heroes share. However, given the Protestant framework of Spenser's work with its inherent view of life as a necessary trial in which the Christian is tested through suffering, his texts emphasize the necessity of resisting the impulse to escape.

The rhetorical and formulaic quality of Redcrosse's reply to Despair's vehement urging to prefer "sleepe" to "toyle" (1.9.40) signals Redcrosse's lack of spiritual energy and unpreparedness to fight his crucial fight against despair. While Despair's discourse is characterized by a skilful use of rhetorical devices, rich imagery, and haunting internal music, Redcrosse's reply takes only a few lines in stanza 41. Platitudinous in tone and vocabulary, it recalls Pythagoras's famous statement, as reported by Cicero in his *De Senectude* 20.73, that man should never depart his station, until his commander tells him to do so.[77] After he has repeated this traditional argument in a colourless and

---

sixteenth-century divines to dispel fear of death by depicting the benefits it offers.

[76] The term "ease" is used at line 9 of stanza 38 and at lines 2, 6 and 9 of stanza 40. In his 1997 edition of the *FQ*, Hamilton argues that "The echoing seas/Ease, rounded out with please characterizes the highly rhetorical nature of the commonplaces used by Despair" (126). That "ease" rhymes with "please" is suggestive of Despair's temptation to avoid effort.

[77] This classical view had become commonplace in religious discourses: cf. for example Calvin's description of life as "a sentry post at which the Lord has posted us, which we must hold until he recalls us" (1: 716). As regards the rhetorical quality of Despair's speech, Harold Skulsky in his *Spenser Encyclopedia* article "Despair" analyses carefully its "verbal schemes" and its "schemes of thought" (213). See also the very good study of the vocabulary

impersonal way, he no longer tries to combat or resist Despair: despair has won his soul. What he had scornfully termed an "idle speach" (st. 31) is a lethal weapon that hits Spenser's disarmed Christian.

The remaining part of the psychomachia described in this canto consists of Redcrosse's progressive yielding to his sense of guilt, fear of God's wrath and doubts about his own election dramatized in the text as Despair's more and more pressing deplorations of Redcrosse's sinfulness and helplessness, and presentation of voluntary death as a sensible (and inescapable) choice in his situation. Redcrosse's silence is a very effective dramatic device that makes Spenser's treatment of the conventional theme so superior to those in his sources. When compared to the pedant verbosity of Thomas Becon's Christian Knight in *The Dialogue between the Christian Knight and Satan* whose faith never wavers, who knows his catechism by heart, and opposes long doctrinal tirades to Satan's arguments, or Epaphroditus's loquacity and readiness to assimilate the good advice offered by his neighbours assembled at his death-bed in Becon's *Sicke Mannes Salue*, or Magnificence's reiterated expressions of regret at having his "life misused" in Skelton's morality play (202), Redcrosse's silence successfully functions, I suggest, to develop pathos by creating expectations of a tragic outcome. It also serves to draw readers' sympathy to Redcrosse, whose silence is a sign of weakness and confusion. From Redcrosse's last words in stanza 41 (or 42 in some readings) to stanza 51 where he raises his armed hand to hit himself, there develops a climax to his spiritual crisis marked by a rhythmic crescendo produced by Despair's more and more pressing questions.[78] The pressing rhythm of Despair's

---

and figures of speech of *FQ* 1.9 in Crampton's excellent *The Condition of Creatures: Suffering and Action in Chaucer and Spenser*, 124-26.

[78] In his 1977 edition of the *FQ* Hamilton remarks that there is no critical agreement as to whether Despair or Redcrosse speaks stanza 42 (127). I personally think that its rhetorical quality is more characteristic of Despair's speech than of that of Redcrosse (it continues the pattern of pressing questions followed by lapidary statements that is distinctive of Despair's discourse). However, doubts about the identity of the speaker seem to me proof

successive arguments seems not to allow Redcrosse enough time to think and answer; he is more and more "charmed" with Despair's "inchaunted rimes" (st. 48). His silence contrasts with the answers Thomas Becon's model Christian in the *Dialogue* gives to Satan whose arguments agree in content, language and arrangement with those of Despair.[79]

Despair presents Redcrosse's sins as irremediable and unforgivable: he has deserted Una, has loved the false Duessa and has shed blood.[80] Redcrosse, this "man of sin" (st. 46), cannot expect mercy or forgiveness from a wrathful God, because "the greater sin, the greater punishment" (st. 43).[81] An immoderate sorrow for sins, loathing of self and above all a failure of faith in God's free saving Grace characterized despairing souls in religious treatises, sermons and personal writings. Thomas Whythorne, a sixteenth-century musician who in his autobiography maintains he has more than once been a victim of despair, describes how the devil makes people feel overwhelmed by the burden of sins:

> So will he present unto us whatsoever we have done and committed against the commandments of God, and will put into our minds huge mountains, as it were, of sins that by the

---

of Spenser's skill, since this submersion of identities suggests Redcrosse's identification with Despair.

[79] This is not surprising, given that Becon reproduces well-established patterns. Some of the arguments used by Becon's Satan which correspond to those of Despair are quoted in notes 80 and 81 below.

[80] In Becon's *Dialogue*, Satan blames the Knight for being "covetuous, proud, lecherous, [. . .] ready unto anger, intemperate, and altogether given to pleasures" and tells him "it is therefore in vain that thou prayest. [. . .] Thou must needs despair" (632, 626).

[81] "Satan: 'Make God's ears deaf with thy prayers so long as thou wilt, yet canst thou never be throughly persuaded and truly believe that thou art heard and shalt be saved; for the righteous only shall be saved'"; Becon's Knight replies: "if we confess our sins, God is faithful and righteous, that he will forgive us our sins, and make us clean from all unrighteousness" (*Dialogue* 626, 630).

outrageousness and greatness of them he may bring us into desperation, which do stagger and doubt of God's mercy and pardon. (125)

If sins are a burden Redcrosse's conscience can hardly bear, Despair's assertion, based on the argument, faultless from the point of view of human logic, that the number of sins increases in direct proportion to the length of one's life, fills Redcrosse with "trembling horror," while his soul is seized by "hellish anguish" (1.9.49). The perspective seems unbearable to him and makes him see death as the only way to interrupt the endless series of sins deserving punishment that leads him to the terrible suffering of despair. Such a perception of death as the only efficacious measure to prevent the multiplication of sins, was sufficiently common for John Sym to list it among the main causes of self-murder:

> The fourth generall motive of men to self-murder, is prevention of sin to come; which a man conceives will inevitably be effected to God's dishonour, and his owne disgrace, if he still live; and may by his death be prevented: and therefore doth he hasten and inflict the same with his owne hands. (237)

Some centuries earlier St. Augustine had already included this motive among those most frequently cited to excuse self-destruction. In Augustine's view it is unlawful to commit a crime in order to prevent further sinning; the absurd logic of such a way of thinking would lead all to commit suicide soon after baptism.[82]

The representation of life as a succession of sins was widely used in religious writings belonging to the two genres of the *contemptus mundi* and the *ars moriendi*, by Catholics and Protestants alike, to help believers overcome their natural fear of death by presenting the advan-

---

[82] "Is it not better to commit such a sin as repentance may purge, than such a one as leaves no place at all for repentance?" (Augustine, *City of God* 1: 29). Book 1, ch. 24 bears the significant title "That sin is not to be avoided by sin."

tages it offers. John Bradford, the Protestant preacher, provides a fine example of the rhetoric of such praise of death in "A Meditation of Death, and the commodities it bringeth":

> What other thing do we daily in this present life, than heap sin to sin, and hoard up trespass upon trespass? So that this day is worse always than yesterday, by increasing, as days, so sins, and therefore thy indignation, good Lord, against us. But when we shall be let go out of the prison of the body, and so taken into thy blessed company, then shall we be in most safety of immortality and salvation. [. . .] The longer in this life thou dost remain, the more thou sinnest, which will turn to thy more pain. (*Sermons and Meditations* 195)[83]

The striking similarity between Bradford's words and Despair's, points to the thin line between two utterly different consequences of the same view of life, one being a serene acceptance of death or at least a diminished fear of it, the other the decision to commit suicide. What makes the difference is of course faith in God's mercy, its presence making Christians joyfully look beyond this 'vale of tears,' its absence leading to despair.

Redcrosse's guilt makes him sink deeper into the pit of self-murdering despair, absorbed by "the vgly vew of his deformed crimes" (1.9.48).[84] It is easy for Despair to finish him off by showing him a picture representing hell and "damned ghosts, that doe in torments waile, / And thousand feends that doe them endlesse paine /

---

[83] This is a lesson that the most popular devotional writings reiterated very often; cf. Becon's assertion that "we cannot cease to sin except we die: why do we then not haste to flee from so great an evil?" (*Sicke Mannes Salue* 148).

[84] Cf. Becon's Knight's exemplary attitude when he says:
I am sorry that so great infirmity reigneth in me; yet do I not therefore despair, but put all my trust in Christ, doubting nothing at all but that he will forgive me my trespasses, and increase my faith daily more and more, that I may inhibit, knock down, quench, oppress, crucify, and kill the works of the flesh. (*Dialogue* 632)

With fire and brimstone" (st. 49). It is a vision often evoked in sermons to make people repent, but it has a devastating effect on Redcrosse's troubled conscience. Sure of his damnation, and to put an end to his unbearable torture, he "At last resolu'd to worke his finall smart, / He lifted vp his hand, that backe againe did start" (st. 51). Having reached the stage that must precede conversion, viz, having gained awareness of his sinful nature and helplessness, Redcrosse should invoke mercy and Grace, instead he loses hope, despairs and chooses to commit the "most monstruous, barbarous, and most vnnaturall" act which "no Beast (be it neuer so sauage and cruell) will do" (Strode 244).[85]

Given contemporary views of suicide, it is reasonable to assume that Redcrosse's act would have aroused a sense of horror in Spenser's readers. But at the same time the crescendo of moral and physiological suffering that characterizes Redcrosse's progressive surrender to despair would seem designed to encourage sympathy for him. Following Despair's long enumeration of Redcrosse's errors and more and more pressing exhortations to shorten the painful wait for his eternal punishment (stanzas 43-47), Redcrosse is "much enmoued" (st. 48). Despair's words "as a swords point through his hart did perse, / And in his conscience made a secret breach" (st. 48). "The vgly vew of his deformed crimes, / [. . .] his manly powres it did disperse" to the extent that "he quakt, and fainted oftentimes" (st. 48). "Whiles trembling horror did his conscience dant, / And hellish anguish did his soule assaile," Despair "shew'd him painted in a table plaine" (st. 49) the endless torments prepared for him in hell, "The sight whereof so throughly him dismaid, / That nought but death before his eyes he saw" (st. 50).

The Spenserian strategy of encouraging at the same time sympathy for the person who commits suicide and horror for the act (see the dramatizations of Terwin's love-melancholy and grisly appearance in

---

[85] Strode's harsh condemnation of suicide is representative of early modern secular views of the moral stigma attached to suicide. Strode was a barrister.

death at 1.9.30 and 36, and of Amavia's toils and ghastly wound at 2.1.50-55 and 40) is employed at its best in stanza 51. Redcrosse is represented in the act of accepting "a dagger sharpe and keene," apt, that is, to produce a deep wound; then his intention is indicated, "At last resolu'd to worke his finall smart"; and his self-murderous movement closes the stanza, "He lifted vp his hand, that backe againe did start" (1.9.51). But as the dramatic action reaches its climax, so does the pathos Spenser has developed in the preceding stanzas. Before the dramatization of Redcrosse's deep emotional and physical trouble, readers cannot but sympathize:

> [. . .] his hand did quake,
> And tremble like a leafe of Aspin greene,
> And troubled bloud through his pale face was seene
> To come, and goe with tydings from the hart,
> As it a running messenger had beene. (1.9.51)

This is where Spenser outdoes by far Skelton or Becon whose despairing characters are not put through such moral and physical ordeals.[86] Significantly the emphasis in Una's address to her suicidal champion falls on the alliterative appellatives "fraile, feeble, fleshly wight" (1.9.53) which evoke the spiritual weakness and the frailties inherent in Redcrosse's passionate fleshly self. Spenser is fond of such alliterative triplets to describe Redcrosse's fall and at the same time draw readers' sympathy to him: at 1.7.11 the narrator describes Redcrosse who prepares to face Orgoglio as "disarmd, disgrast, and inwardly dismayde"; at 1.7.51 Una echoes this description in her report to Ar

---

[86] See for instance the dramatic superiority of Redcrosse's silence after Una has snatched the knife from his hand, which functions as a sign of his confusion and trouble, compared to Skelton's dramatization of Magnyficence's prompt and articulate thanks to Good Hope who has snatched the knife he held (*Magnificence* 204, vv. 2328 and 2332-35). Spenser's representation of Redcrosse's suffering is reminiscent of contemporary medical descriptions of the mental and physiological alterations affecting melancholy people.

thur of Orgoglio's victory over her "disarmed, dissolute, dismaid" champion.

When he accepts the dagger from Despair's hands, Redcrosse is already agonizing, dying from a self-inflicted moral and spiritual wound. Certainly he does not proudly stand, brave and bold, like those classical heroes, so often described in noble terms as they enact their absolute freedom and dignity through suicide. Redcrosse is a defeated Everyman who has become fully aware of his human insufficiency, but is incapable of asking God to compensate for it by his omnipotence. It is God's gratuitous grace, whose vehicle Una is, that catches the knight on the brink of the gulf of damnation. Assuming the role that in *Magnificence* is Good Hope's, Una stops Redcrosse's suicidal hand by urging him to trust in "heauenly mercies" and reminds him that being "chosen" he should not despair (1.9.53).[87] Uncertainty about one's election was always mentioned among the main causes of despair in religious writings. It is central, for instance, in George Abbot's address to an imaginary despairing Christian, whose temptations and ungodly thoughts are identical to those of Redcrosse:

> Whosoever thou are that groanest under this heavy burthen, strengthen thy feeble knees, and resume thy decaying spirits. If the motions of thy mind be fearful beyond measure, yea unfit to be spoken and uttered by thee, so that thou art ashamed even to name them– ... that thy sins shall not be forgiven thee, that thou belongest not to God's election, that the promises of his mercy appertain to other men, but are not true

---

[87] Note the parallelism between Una's gesture at 1.9.52 and Duessa's at 1.7.14: Una stops Redcrosse's lifted suicidal hand, and thus saves him from damnation; Duessa stops the lifted hand of Orgoglio who is about to dispatch Redcrosse (she does so by entreating him to "hold [his] mortal hand for Ladies sake," and by offering herself as "worthy meed," 1.7.14) not because she wishes to save the knight, but so that he can remain forever Orgoglio's "bondslaue" (st. 14), viz, a slave to his own fleshly self, a prisoner of the "old man" in him.

in thee, that thy best way were to despatch thyself of thy life by some fall, or a knife, or by drowning or otherwise, since thou art but a forlorn person and a cast-away in God's sight (which is a most fearful and uncomfortable thought), [. . .] know that thou herein art not alone: such conflicts are very common. (267)

The cure Abbot suggests for this suicidal Christian is the same Becon, Coverdale, Perkins, and many other Protestant churchmen prescribed to those who were experiencing despair, either in the course of life or on the deathbed: prayers; trust in God's promise and mercy; repentance; and penance. This is exactly Redcrosse's spiritual itinerary in the House of Holiness, and it is not an easy or painless one as we learn from his relapse into suicidal thoughts.

Having experienced more than once an overwhelming desire of death as annihilation of temptations and afflictions, a desire that in Spenser's day, as we have seen, was the object of philosophical and theological censure, Redcrosse is finally admitted to the House of Holiness, where both Una and the reader would expect him to learn the lesson of Christian patience and endurance. There Una hopes her champion, who at present is too "feeble" and "faint" (1.10.2) to embrace life in all its complexity and toilsomeness, will be restored to physical and psychological wholesomeness; translated into theological terms, Una expects Redcrosse will become a "new man." Yet, even as a "new man" Redcrosse manifests a propensity to fall prey to exhaustion and impatience. This is apparent when he expresses death-wishes on the Mount of Contemplation and during the battle with the dragon. The persistence of Redcrosse's unorthodox death-wish, even in his regenerate state, testifies to the power and persistence of the "old man."

When the narrator describes the stages in Redcrosse's long training in "perfection of heauenly grace" (1.10.21) in the House of Holiness, he mentions the crucial moments when the knight "that wretched world [. . .] gan for to abhore, / And mortall life gan loath, as thing forlore," desiring "to end his wretched dayes" (st. 21).[88] The boundary line between the renunciation of earthly things tirelessly preached by the church and a reprehensible attitude of active rejection of the world seems at times to be extremely thin. This is why theologians and moralists in their frequent treatments of the desire of death unhesitatingly condemned the death-wish arising from "loathing of life" as ungodly and unchristian (Perkins, *Salve* 1: 513).[89] Similarly, Una is "assayld with great perplexitie" when she sees her champion in "this distressed doubtfull agonie," "disdeining life, desiring leaue to die" (1.10.22): she realizes Redcrosse's is not an orthodox Christian death-wish, it is less an aspiration to be admitted among God's saints, than loathing of self and life.[90] The efforts of Fidelia and Patience, Amendment and Penance and all the other "physicians of the soul" displace these unholy escapist inclinations only momentarily. Soon Redcrosse's apparent propensity to desire death appears again twice, first within the frame of Christian orthodoxy on the Mount of Contemplation, then as a yearning for relief from pain and toil during his fight with the dragon.

When on the Mount of Contemplation Redcrosse finally discovers his own identity and learns he will become Saint George, patron of England, his first reaction is one of sadness at the idea of having to leave "deeds of armes" and "Ladies loue," behind, but soon his regret

---

[88] Elizabeth Heale describes the "paradigm of salvation" as contemporary Protestant theology saw it (21). One of its crucial elements is contempt of self and a view of the world as not an end in itself, a point of arrival, but as a necessary and yet transitional stage within the redemptive process. Redcrosse, instead, inclines to stop there.

[89] See also Calvin's commendation of "contempt of the present life that engenders no hatred of it" (1: 716).

[90] A propensity to excessive introspection and self-loathing still characterizes Redcrosse even after his stay at the House of Holiness; when Una welcomes him back, she urges him "himselfe to chearish, and consuming thought / To put away out of his carefull brest" (1.10.29). The risk inhering in the Protestant insistence on the necessity for believers to explore the depths of their guilt and corruption in order to become receptacles for Grace is alluded to.

vanishes as Contemplation reminds him that mundane things are all "vaine, and vanish into nought" (1.10.62). Immediately Redcrosse says he would rather embrace contemplative life and leave the active, "let me here for aye in peace remaine" (st. 63), but it is clear his is not a holy aspiration to a life which, though devoted to contemplation, is nonetheless as active as that of the Spenserian hermits who are always ready to act as spiritual guides and healers; it is instead a desire of withdrawal, of disengagement, in fact all he wants is "peace." His is still mainly a negative attitude of rejection of the world due to its shortcomings and failure to live up to expectations. Besides, his contemplation of the fruitful joys of the Kingdom of God has made him unwilling "to turne againe / Backe to the world, whose ioyes so fruitlesse are" (st. 63). Instead of actively trying to promote God's kingdom on earth, Redcrosse would retire to cultivate his contempt-of-the-world mood.

Redcrosse falls prey to a temptation Spenser presents as frequent and common: the temptation to abandon one's quest arising from exhaustion, a sense of the futility of human pursuits and a desire to stop undergoing life's painful and seemingly purposeless trials. Redcrosse is as weary as Calidore, the knight of Courtesy, and would probably subscribe to his vision of active life as a difficult navigation in "seas of troubles and of toylesome paine" (6.9.31). But, if Spenser's texts lay stress on the toil and suffering any quest implies, yet they also emphasize the necessity of not yielding to the temptation to desert duty and immure oneself in a futile life that is a living death.

Redcrosse, then, like all the other Spenserian characters who long for rest and oblivion, is urged to hold out and complete the assigned quest whose difficulty and painfulness are never withheld from him. In fact, he is told by Contemplation he will enjoy "ioyous rest and endlesse blis" only after "labours long, and sad delay" (1.10.52). Even when he finally expresses an orthodox Christian death-wish, a holy desire of admission to "the immediate fellowship of Christ and God himselfe in heaven" (Perkins, *Salve* 513), in Redcrosse's words a desire to "streight way on that last long voyage fare" (st. 63), the knight relapses into escapist impulses and would leave the world at once. Contemplation has to remind him that he has not yet fulfilled his duty as Christian warrior. The lesson Contemplation teaches Redcrosse recalls St. Paul's difficult decision to postpone the fulfillment of his godly desire of death until his duty on earth is completely done:

> For I am greatly in doubt on both sides, desiring to bee loosed and to bee with Christ, which is best of all. Neverthelesse, to abide in the flesh, is more needefull for you. And this am I sure of, that I shal abide, and with you all continue, for your furtherance and ioy of your faith. (Phil. 1.23-25)

Once returned to the world of his quest, however, Redcrosse shows he has not assimilated Contemplation's teachings about the duties inhering in his own role and is still ignorant of the difference between a godly death-wish arising from the desire to enjoy "the fellowship of Christ" and an ungodly death-wish caused by impatience with the toil and pain which are the common lot of any "man of earth" (1.10.52). As soon as he leaves the Mount, in fact, he relapses into his own old habit of desiring death as escape when life seems unbearably distressing. During his battle with the dragon, we are informed, "death did he oft desire" (1.11.28): his loss of will to live arises from exhaustion and impatience.[91] Redcrosse is "faint, wearie, sore, emboyled, grieued, brent / With heat, toyle, wounds, armes, smart, and inward fire" (st. 28). He is "faint," "wearie" and "grieued" as so many other Spenserian characters are, and like them feels he cannot bear life's "toyle" and "wounds" any longer.

Redcrosse's death-wish arises from his loathing of himself as a fallen mortal, subject to needs, perturbations, and desires that con-

---

[91] The majority of theologians in Spenser's day might well have deemed Redcrosse's death-wish no less "faultie" than those of Job, Jeremiah and Jonas who "failed herein because they desired death being carried away with impatience" (Perkins, *Salve* 513).

stantly expose him to frustration, suffering, and sin. One should not forget that during the first day of battle against the dragon (which of course figures forth Satan or evil), Redcrosse is no match for it and is almost destroyed. Having lost hope in the battle for salvation, Redcrosse once again desires death.[92] Through death Redcrosse wants to get rid of his corruptible self, of the body which "created in the likeness of God and thus in perfection, has become through the Fall the chief weapon in the armoury of sin and death" (Leslie 110).[93] But as the narrative shows, to get rid of the earthly portion of the self is not what brings salvation. It is not the rejection of this portion, but its transformation that initiates the process.[94] Hence Redcrosse becomes a "new-borne knight" (st. 34) after his immersion in the Well of Life; his armour is hardened and made fit to withstand the dragon's blows.[95]

When during the first day of battle Redcrosse relies on himself, he is beaten and the apprehension of his own insufficiency and vulnerability drives him to despair. Absorbed in exhaustion, self-loathing and desire "his armes to leaue" (1.11.26), he does not realize that gaining awareness of his frailty and the insufficiency of his own resources, has been a necessary step towards becoming a receptacle of God's grace. The narrative, then, signals how reliance on human strength to face life's battles is foolish and exposes the individual to failure and despair. Life's dark meanders are like Mammon's underworld dwelling in Book 2 of the *Faerie Queene*, a place of labour and strife, the house of temptation and desire; walking through them with no spiritual guide, unaided by Grace, necessarily makes people faint out of ex-

---

[92] Redcrosse "thought his [. . .] helmet to vnlace" (1.11.26); in St. Paul a knight without his helmet emblematizes the Christian who has abandoned hope (1 Thess. 5.8).

[93] The idea of the mortification of the "old man" or sinful mortal self in us is certainly suggested here. Since this idea emerges more clearly in Spenser's treatment of the "living dead," I will discuss it in more detail in Chapter 7 below.

[94] Maleger's narrative develops this view; see Chapter 7 below.

[95] For a discussion of the significance of the Well of Life, see Hume 103-105.

haustion, their physical, moral, and spiritual energies being all spent. *The Faerie Queene* represents living as a descent into the mortal body, an exposure to the temptations, desires, perturbations, and trials attendant on mortal life. If one passes through life unaccompanied, relying only on oneself, one faints. One needs faith and Grace, as Sir Guyon needs the Angel and Redcrosse the water of the Well and the balm from the Tree of Life, to revive and regain strength.

The narrative of Redcrosse's death-wish during the battle is one of the many instances when Spenser depicts people yearning for relief from life through death which is seen less as a new birth, than as an end, the end of what they loathe above everything else, that is, life and the trials that occasion their becoming fully aware of their own frailty and insufficiency. Having related how the knight "death did [. . .] oft desire," Spenser's narrator adds a reflection which expresses regret and bitterness: "But death will neuer come, when needes require" (1.11.28).[96] The expression "needes require" seems to suggest the idea that some sufferings are so terrible that they make death appear as the only answer to a very human need. Although the wrong answer in a Christian perspective as the context makes it clear, this kind of death-wish is presented as the natural and unsurprising desire of a despairing "man of earth" (1.10.52). Redcrosse is just one in a group of "faint" and "wearie" (1.11.28) death-wishers in the *Faerie Queene* who cannot see their suffering as a "loving visitation of God" (Becon, *Sicke Mannes Salue* 94) who, by offering them the opportunity to become fully aware of the frailty and corruption inherent in their nature as "old men," prepares their transformation into "new men."

---

[96] Cf. Boethius: "Death, happy to men when she does not intrude in the sweet years, but comes when often called in sorrow, turns a deaf ear to the wretched and cruelly refuses to close weeping eyes" (3).

5. Death as Escape from Suffering

Not a few Spenserian characters share Redcrosse's view of death as the only efficacious remedy for physical or moral sufferings that seem unbearable. Just like Redcrosse both before and after his encounter with Contemplation, they tend to see and desire death as a release from the toils and frustrations of life. This is exactly the kind of death-wish contemporary religious orthodoxy condemned. A couple of examples taken from popular and influential tracts will give an idea of the theological attitude. At the close of a passage designed to illustrate what makes desire of death lawful and godly, George Abbot specifies that under certain circumstances the desire to be "out of life" is a sin:

> [. . .] if they be but froward thoughts and wearying perturbations which distemper us too much, or if it be for some sorrows and afflictions which fall on us, [. . .] then in wishing for death we prove plainly to be offenders. (260)

Similarly, John Sym declares that when "eager desire" of death "is more for *freedome* from some temporary evills; than for to enjoy spirituall and eternall good," this desire is undoubtedly "sinfull" (258).

Theologians, however, were not the only critics of escapist inclinations generated by weariness with existential hardships. Philosophers, especially those who were the promoters and interpreters of a renewed interest in Stoicism, insisted that the wise man should never be deeply troubled and disheartened because of life's blows. Thus Lipsius, one of the most widely read and influential thinkers of the Renaissance, devotes two chapters of his major work (*Two Bookes of Constancie*, Book 1, chs. 21 and 22) to presentation of and comment upon Seneca's idea of the necessity to learn and practise the art of remaining imperturbed even when facing tribulations.[97] Indeed, the Renaissance was enthusiastic in its reception of centuries-old Stoic teachings like

---

[97] Here is how Seneca thinks the wise man should face life: "Let fate find us ready and unafraid. It's the great soul that surrenders itself to fate" (letter 107.12, 2: 221). On Lipsius see Part I, note 20.

those of Boethius who in the *Consolation of Philosophy* (written in 524 A.D.) exhorts people to be stronger than adversities. He suggests the wise man should never give in to despair when hard times come, in imitation of the "brave soldier" who, not "intimidated by the noise of battle," fights "manfully against any fortunes, neither despairing in the face of misfortune nor becoming corrupt in the enjoyment of prosperity" (99).

Such theological and philosophical attitudes are, however, rarely dramatized in *The Faerie Queene*. One looks almost in vain in Spenser's work for characters championing Stoic or Christian serenity and the brave acceptance of life's turmoils (the hermit of Book 6 is perhaps the only proper exception). Instead, we are offered a rich gallery of portraits of utterly dejected people. Significantly, it is not just the weak or the ungodly who, when facing trials, despair and desire to die; even Una, that living emblem of virtue, piety and courage, calls upon death as an escape from her overwhelming grief when she thinks Redcrosse is dead.[98]

The group of those unable or unwilling to bear afflictions with patience, and making death the object of their longing is large and heterogeneous. Some are hurt in their body, others in their soul, and others experience both physical and moral pain at the same time. Some sufferers are the victims of circumstances, others are themselves the cause of their own woes. Beyond these differences, however, there is a crucial common feature: all react to trials with a fervent desire to die.

Enough has been said above of Redcrosse's paradigmatical incapacity to endure physical and moral sufferings with patience and refrain from wishing himself immediately delivered of life. Another character who reacts in the same way is Phedon who murders friend and fiancée

---

[98] Abbot was otherwise not very indulgent with human frailties, but he admits that even God's saints can be tempted to curse and reject life, desiring its end mainly for the sake of release from tribulations. He gives as an example Jeremiah's express wish that "he had never been, or would that he had been slain at first entering into the world (Jer. 20.14)" (267). Una's reaction to woe is discussed in Chapter 9 below which deals with bereavement.

II The Psychology of Despair 77

out of jealousy. Phedon's sufferings are the result of his own misdoings and are thus in a sense self-inflicted like those of Redcrosse in Orgoglio's dungeon and Despair's cave. Chased and beaten by Furor, the embodiment of his own state of mind at the time of his crimes, Phedon is referred to significantly as "the thral of wretchednesse" (2.4.16) by his rescuer, Guyon. This is not just another way of saying that he is "that caitiues [Furor] thral" as the comma between the two expressions in the same line apparently suggests. Phedon is really the "thral" of the "wretchednesse" he has prepared for himself, he is imprisoned in a state of torment that makes his life a living hell.

Phedon's torment is generated by the memory of his deeds, the remorse and grief that, as he confesses to Guyon, never leave him. With "throbbing" heart and "watry" eyes he declares he has not only heaped "crime on crime," thus exposing himself to the distress deriving from a guilty conscience, but also "griefe on griefe" (2.4.17, 31). In fact, even though he is their murderer, since he loved friend and fiancée dearly, he feels bereaved, hence he suffers from the absence of his loved ones and experiences the sense of loss typical of bereavement, "to losse of loue adioyning losse of frend" (st. 31). Not surprisingly, he sees his own death as the only way out of the spiritual and emotional maze he is in. "Death were better, then such agony, / As griefe and furie vnto me did bring": he thinks only death can obliterate the "mortall sting" he feels in his heart and soul, a sting that "during life will neuer be appeasd" (2.4.33). What he longs for is the cessation of grief, together with the annihilation of those faculties (memory, moral sensibility, conscience) which make him feel the burden of guilt and remorse. Like Redcrosse, Phedon yearns for death as release from his sinful self; both see erasure of the self as the only way to escape guilt.

It should be noticed that Phedon never includes the possibility of having become the object of divine wrath and being destined to eternal punishment among thoughts tormenting him. Although these preoccupations are likely to be implied in his references to his sense of guilt and remorse, they are significantly not even mentioned in passing.

Like the vast majority of Spenserian grieving characters, with the notable exception of Redcrosse, Phedon is so obsessed with and totally absorbed by his present situation, the temporary living hell he is experiencing in the here and now, that he seems to be unconcerned with or unable to concentrate on the perspective of the eternal. This signals that his vision is earthbound. Within the Christian frame of reference of *The Faerie Queene*, in fact, it is pure folly to desire to be released from temporary torments at the cost of gaining the eternal. This happens when the earthly experience is not set against the background of the celestial. As the context of Spenser's narratives of death-desires makes clear, the trouble with a perspective such as that of Phedon is not only that it is ungodly, but that it leads people to despair.

Phedon is neither openly criticized for his incapacity to bear afflictions with patience nor rebuked for his escapist desire of death. Instead, he is shown sympathy and is spoken to in a compassionate tone by Guyon who, far from highlighting his weakness and condemning him for his crimes (Phedon has already done this himself), concentrates on the means to alleviate his suffering and endeavours to convince him that temperance can cure his "hurts" (2.4.33). As a remedy against despair and loss of will to live, Guyon proposes that Phedon concentrate on his life and take active steps to reform it. He exhorts him to check immoderate "wrath, gealosie, griefe, loue" (st. 35) in order to avoid falling again prey to them and becoming the object of his own hatred by acting on them. Reformation, not death, is the way out of despair and self-loathing.

Another character for whom death is a deliverance from a tormenting self is Pyrochles who longs for the moment when the passions and inclinations he cannot master and which make his life a living hell will be quenched once and for all. The son of Acrates (Intemperance) and Despight, Pyrochles embodies wrath; he himself describes the nature and degree of his suffering, when he says he is so possessed and tormented by an "implacable" "inly" "fire," that he sees death as a healer (2.6.44).[99]

Unlike Redcrosse or Phedon, Pyrochles is to be seen both as a character figuring forth a suffering individual, and as a personification of a passion, wrath. He also dramatizes the impulse of some Spenserian characters to shed their mortal selves as a way of freeing themselves from passion. Hence the reiteration of subject and verb in his reply to his varlet's enquiry about the reasons for his resolve to drown himself: "I burne, I burne, I burne" (2.6.44). His words signify at the same time the anguish and exasperation of those who feel eaten alive, consumed by passions they cannot master, and Pyrochles' function as personification of the physical and psychological imbalance arising from an excess of choleric humour. If Spenser's text often dwells on the consequences in terms of torment and despair of the frustrated desires and violent passions which beset the death-wishers, here it stages the destructive potential of passion itself, indicated by the multiple references to fire and flames and their consuming power.

Pyrochles cries he is "burning in flames" no "sea of licour cold, nor lake of mire" can quench since, as he realizes, they are invisible, "inly," that is moral, not physical, "Burning in flames, yet no flames can I see" (2.6.45, 44). Significantly, like Redcrosse in Orgoglio's dungeon, Pyrochles describes himself as suffering a living death, unable to find release from life in death, "dying daily, daily yet reuiue" (st. 45). Once again, consideration of Pyrochles' double status is crucial. He seems both mortal, a tormented individual who longs to die as Redcrosse and Phedon do, but as a personification he embodies, in particularly extreme form, the inherent miseries and guilt of human flesh subjected to passion. As an individual like all those who chal-

---

[99] "Fire" here clearly points to the heat that characterizes the choleric humour As John Webster and Richard Isomaki in their *Spenser Encyclopedia* article on Pyrochles and Cymochles remark, the name Pyrochles, "from Greek *pyr* (fire) and *ochleō* (to move, trouble, or disturb by tumult) [. . .] suggests volatility and wrathfulness" (574).

lenge Arthur he seems susceptible to being killed, but as a personification of passion, he cannot die, because desire and passion are inherent in mortality.

Pyrochles declares his plight is worse than that afflicting any "damned ghoste / In flaming *Phlegeton*"; he feels hell is really in this life. He feels only physical death can heal his moral and psychological sickness: "Nothing but death can doe me to respire" (2.6.50, 44). And his death-desire is so strong, that when his varlet plunges into the water to rescue him, the two find themselves striving for two opposite goals: "the one himselfe to drowne, / The other both from drowning for to saue" (st. 47). Spenser's narrative represents the desire for death, viz, the impulse to shed one's mortal self, as at times prevailing over the motive of self-preservation in those who are unable to check excesses of passions which are felt as torment.

Soon after he is prevented from drowning himself, Pyrochles again falls prey to suicidal urges. When the victorious Arthur at the end of a furious fight offers to spare his life, Pyrochles disdainfully refuses, urging the prince to kill him and let people know that he has not died "ouercome" (2.8.52), but of his own free will. He asks Arthur to make known this declaration that he "in despight of life, for death do[th] call" (st. 52). In my view, the idea suggested here is that of wilful human agency in furthering the sequence of passion-torment-despair-desire of death. Pyrochles' "willful self-destructiveness" (Webster and Isomaki 574), on which the narrative clearly focuses, dramatizes human responsibility for the destruction of one's own psychological, moral and spiritual resources when one lets the corruptible and mortal in oneself prevail, when one leads the life of the flesh.[100]

---

[100] Webster and Isomaki point out that Pyrochles' "motto, 'Burnt I do burne' (iv 38), captures his willful self-destructiveness, and even before Pyrochles himself appears, his squire Atin creates a picture of him as a knight who wills himself to act even when he has neither cause nor object" (574). At 2.5.1 the narrator remarks that Pyrochles is "his owne woes authour" and at 2.8.52 he says that Pyrochles "wilfully refused grace."

II The Psychology of Despair 81

Pyrochles' rejection of life is absolute and irrevocable; now that he is about to obtain at last a long sought for death, he lets nothing and no one come between him and the object of his desire. One immediately recalls another expression in Spenser of equally intense desire of death and fear of being prevented from obtaining that release: it is the dying words of the suicide Amavia to Sir Guyon who strives to revive her: "Take not away now got, which none would giue to me" (2.1.47). Blind to the fact that they could make their torments tolerable by mastering the excesses of their passions (anger for Pyrochles, grief for Amavia), both expect the death of their torments from death which appears merely as the end of something, not as a fresh start.[101]

A fourth character whose story, like those of Redcrosse, Phedon and Pyrochles, develops the theme of desire for death as a release from moral and psychological suffering, is Timias who not only spends his days in Book 4, canto 7 entreating death to come, but also refuses to care for himself hoping thus to shorten a life he loathes. At first sight Timias might seem just another of those melancholy lovers crowding Elizabethan sonnet sequences, but the narrator makes clear that the causes of his distress go beyond mere love-sickness. Separated from Belphoebe who has unjustly accused him of unfaithfulness, it is the "fowle dishonor" (4.7.37) deriving from her accusation that takes away from him his joie de vivre; as Hamilton comments "since Timias's name signifies honour, *dishonor* brings death" (1977 edition of the *FQ* 478).[102] The "wofull wight" retires to a cabin in the depths of the forest and there he turns into the living image of "sad melancholy" (st. 38). His voluntary seclusion and his abandoning of duty and social role (he breaks his "wonted warlike weapons" and throws

---

[101] An interesting reading of the narrative of Pyrochles can be found in Crampton 142-55. Crampton explores Pyrochles' simultaneous role as agent and patient in the *agere-et-pati* pattern underlining Spenser's treatment of anger.

[102] Dishonour, viz loss of queenly favour following his secret marriage to Elizabeth Throckmorton, forces Sir Walter Raleigh (Timias's historical pattern) into the living death of a five-year exile from the court, the place of his social, economic, cultural, and political quests.

them away "with vow to vse no more," st. 39) make him one of the poem's living dead, a state emblematized in his transformed appearance as a "ghost late risen from his graue" (4.8.12).

Throughout Spenser's work, the will to go on living despite adversity usually goes hand in hand with active engagement, with the enthusiastic choice, or at least the voluntary acceptance of, a quest. The text often highlights the tight link between the will to live and the willingness to engage by showing that when people partly or wholly lose the first, they simultaneously shun society (hence the voluntary seclusion of death-wishers like Timias in *The Faerie Queene*, Alcyon in *Daphnaida* and Colin Clout in the *Shepheardes Calender*) and abandon their tasks. Besides, Spenser's narratives frequently develop the view that an individual's quest and active engagement in society are crucial for the development and maintenance of a fully human identity. Significantly, when Redcrosse and Timias abdicate their duties and divest their roles, they become ghost-like, they lose their humanity.[103] Their physical transformation is so radical, friends and lovers hardly recognize them when they meet, thus signifying that Redcrosse and Timias are not themselves any more. Shape-shifting, like such evil characters as Malengin, Proteus, and Archimago, they lack the stability of the virtuous self.

Like Redcrosse, whom Arthur and Una hardly recognize when he emerges from Orgoglio's dungeon, Timias has changed to the point that the persons who are most familiar with him, Arthur and Belphoebe, meet him and even talk to him without realizing whom he is.[104] Having expressed his self-hate and suicidal urges through nearly

---

[103] Spenser fully exploits the repertoire of conventional attributes of the melancholic (love of solitude, indifference to duty, dishevelled appearance, etc.) and makes it the base on which he builds his discourse.

[104] For an earlier instance of this motif of loss of identity through loss of role, see the Medieval romance *Ywain and Gawain*. Ywain, having broken his word to his wife, abandons Arthur and goes to live in the forest; "his identity as a knight has been destroyed, and so he is no more 'Ywain'" (Schmidt and Jacobs 1: 14).

starving himself to death, "The more his weakened body so to wast," he has eventually become a living image of death, a "pale and wan" "pined ghost" (4.7.41, 43). Death in fact is the object of his longing, as he tells Belphoebe, to whom he has finally made himself known. To her he presents himself as one who lives unwillingly. He is yet another of those Spenserian characters who feel they are prisoners of life: his torments, he says, have made him "loath this life, still longing for to die" (4.8.16). Having vowed "in that wildernesse, of men forlore, / [. . .] / His hard mishap in dolor to deplore, / And wast his wretched daies in wofull plight," he spends his life "in dolour and despaire" (4.7.39, 43), weeping and wailing "night and day" (4.8.2). A reiterated use of expressions such as "*wast* his wretched daies," "*wearing out* his youthly yeares," "*wore* away" (4.7.39, 41; 4.8.2; italics mine), emphasizes the motif of waste and of the futility of a life that has lost its godly purpose. Timias's wilful immurement in a useless life that is a living death is condemned by Belphoebe who appropriates the language and the arguments of theology. She says that if Timias's miserable physical and moral state is caused by "inward griefe or wilfull scorne / Of life," then his attitude is censurable

> For he whose daies in wilfull woe are worne,
> The grace of his Creator doth despise,
> That will not vse his gifts for thanklesse nigardise. (4.8.15)

Despite their loss of hope and spiritual insight, Redcrosse, Phedon, and Timias are redeemable figures unlike inhuman "living dead" such as Maleger, Sansjoy, and Malbecco.

6. Living Death and Deathless Life

As we have seen, many of Spenser's grieving or embittered characters describe themselves as living dead imprisoned in a life that is nothing but an endless inner death preceding a greatly desired physical death. The idea of immurement in what appears as a deathless life is as remarkable in *The Faerie Queene* for its emphasis and recurrence as the motif of the death-wish. While the false desire for death that we followed in the previous chapters implies its twinned opposite, a godly desire for death, the apprehension of death in life that I examine in this section serves to contrast a corrupt and mortal experience of life as death with its godly twin, a spiritual view of the life of the flesh as a living death.

Significantly, Spenser often develops rhetorical patterns on the words 'life' and 'death' and their derivatives. Employing a variety of rhetoric schemes, he combines the two words in odd ways, attributes to the one the meaning that is usually associated with the other, and creates word-play and paradoxical statements. *Oxymoron*, *syllepsis* and *polyptoton* are just some of the figures of speech Spenser uses to convey the idea of the frequent exchange of distinctive features between life and death, making life take the place of death. Some examples of such word-play used to emphasize the living deaths of characters are the descriptions of Alcyon who presents himself as one who "liuing thus doo die" (*Daphnaida* 383); of Colin Clout who asks himself "why dyest thou stil, and yet aliue art founde?" (*Shepheardes Calender*, "December" 95); of Maleger who is defined a "dead-liuing swaine" (*FQ* 2.11.44); and of Malbecco who "dying liues" (*FQ* 3.10.60).

It is crucial, I think, to take notice of the difference in purpose between the inversion of the meanings of 'life' and 'death' so typical of scriptural texts and later religious writings, and that found in Spenser's narratives. The beliefs of late Judaism and Christianity are founded on a vision of this life as death, what comes after physical death being the real and only true life. In the light of God's admonition to Adam and

II The Psychology of Despair 85

Eve not to eat the forbidden fruit accompanied with mention of the penalty in case of trespass, "Thou shalt die" (Genesis 2.17), mortal life after the Fall has been identified with death. In fact, since Augustine's warning to early Christians that "this mortal life be rather to be called death than life" (2: 7), the church has never ceased to present life as death in order to persuade people to look away from this life and gaze upon the one to come.[105] Incorporated into the ideology of the Christian West, the view that this life is really a "liuing death, a dying life deseruing rather to be called a true death, then the shadow of death, a shadow of life, then a true life" is given prominence in the writings of churchmen and laymen alike; my quote, in fact, is from a moral tract published in 1618 by George Strode, an English barrister (41).

Obviously well aware of the theological reasoning behind and practical persuasive function of this habitual reversal of the literal meanings of the words 'life' and 'death,' Spenser makes the device serve a different purpose in a perspective that is reduced from the otherwordly to the merely mundane. Whereas Donne, a poet who like Spenser makes extensive use of the paradox, usually refers to life and death in a transcendent perspective as in the subtitle of his most famous sermon, "Death's Duel, or, a consolation to the soul against the dying life and the living death of the body," Spenser moves within more circumscribed bounds. Whenever the meanings of life and death are exchanged in his narratives of living death, the explicit frame of reference is the human condition here and now. It is not so much spiritual perspectives that arouse Spenser's embittered and despairing characters' apprehension of life as death, as rather their impatience in the face of trials and suffering to which they react by opting out of life

---

[105] In Book 13, Chapter 2 of his immensely influential *City of God* Augustine dwells on the idea that as soon as human beings are conceived, they enter death. Chapter 2 bears a revealing title: "Whether One May be Living and Dead both Together" (2: 7). Calvin often reflects on the exchange of significance between life and death that is at the core of Christian theology; the *Institutes* abounds in remarks like this: "And what else is it for us to remain in life but to be immersed in death?" (1: 716).

and immuring themselves in despair or unproductive stasis. This chapter will show that Spenser's rhetorical reversal of the literal meanings of 'life' and 'death' with reference to merely mundane realities, values, and goals, is crucial to his representation of fleshly perspectives as dangerous both for Christians' spiritual wholesomeness and for their psychological balance.

As I suggested earlier, Spenser's grieving characters tend to present themselves as people who live in "liues despight" (*FQ* 2.1.36), living dead who cannot die and live in endless agony. Life to them appears as a terrible, protracted deathless death from which they long to withdraw. Spenser's narratives present this sort of life as the only form of death arousing horror, the only one to be feared. The condition of those who, having lost hope, or faith, or any interest in the world, lead unproductive lives, is dramatized as worse than any other. Compared to this terrible form of spiritual, intellectual, emotional and social living-death, physical death, so often the object of such deep anxiety and revulsion in Spenser's day, is a trifle. In fact, as Kathrine Koller has shown very well, "characters in *The Faerie Queene* accept or deliver death with very little display of emotion" (132): what Spenser presents as really upsetting and terrifying is the life that has lost its godly direction.

Spenser repeatedly emphasizes his despairing characters' paradoxical apprehension of death not as a single, necessarily unique event at the end of life, but as a daily experience that recurs indefinitely. Redcrosse in Orgoglio's dungeon feels he is "dying euery stound" (*FQ* 1.8.38) and the bereaved Alcyon says he "daylie die [. . .]" (*Daphnaida* 435). It is not the Christian perspective of immortal life that makes Spenser's suffering characters see their present life as death, but rather their merely mortal view of life. Unwilling to accept that pain, loss and disillusion are part and parcel of fallen life in a fallen world, they opt out of life, at least momentarily. It is because life is the realm of impermanence and loss that they apprehend it as death, and this signals the earthliness of their view.

Spenser's despairing characters long for that one death that will interrupt the series of their daily deaths; hence they desire physical death mainly as an end, not as a birth. Such characters as Redcrosse and Timias figure human beings trapped in their mortality, hostage to the needs, lusts and passions that inhere in their mortal frame and that nothing earthly can fully or permanently satisfy. Such needs and desires arouse an endless series of torments, dissatisfactions and griefs, that to the eyes of the "old man," the eyes of the flesh rather than of faith, appear as meaningless. Spenser's narratives of living death dramatize the view that when sufferers lose or forget spiritual perspectives, they see trials less as moments of redeeming penance, than as repeated deaths in a deathless, therefore hopeless and aimless life.

In their despair, the Spenserian characters who wilfully immure themselves in a living death, such as Redcrosse and Timias, are described as persons experiencing the torments of hell in this life. They resemble those "trembling ghosts with sad amazed mood, / [. . .] staring wide / With stonie eyes" (1.5.32) which people the classical underworld Spenser so often evokes. Spenser's living dead lead a futile and unproductive existence similar to that of the inhabitants of Hades as Homer describes them in *Odyssey* 2, a "dim multitude" of "phantoms of exhausted humans."[106] Having experienced despair and vainly entreated death to come, Spenser's living dead cease to participate in godly living and assume the aspect and attitude of those liminal creatures, the "wretched ghosts" who are "wailing euermore" (*Virgils Gnat* 384) and whose "restlesse spright[s]" endlessly wander on "Stygian shores" (*FQ* 1.4.48). Like them, they bear the marks of death on their face: when Redcrosse emerges from Orgoglio's dungeon he is a "ruefull spectacle of death," "his sad dull eyes deepe sunck in hollow pits" (1.8.40, 41) and Timias looks like a "pined ghost" (4.7.41).

In fact, all the Spenserian despairing characters are remarkably similar. Redcrosse, Timias, Alcyon, for example, are attributed similar fea-

---

[106] I use Ariès's very effective description of Homer's dead in *Hour of Our Death* 23.

tures not only because they all display the outward marks of melancholy as contemporary literature described them, but also to signify that they are all immured in the life of the flesh that is death. The "old man," viz, the self that is passionate, mortal and sinful, is made visible.[107] Their decayed and diseased bodies signify their imprisonment in mortality and their fleshly apprehension of things. Dead to spiritual meanings, and unwilling to submit to God's providence, they seem to experience hell as some theologians saw it, more a condition of spiritual and moral death than a place of physical torture.[108] Their condition is very much like that of the damned as Augustine describes it when he states that they are neither "before death nor after death, but eternally in death: never living, never dead, but ever dying" (2: 9).

Like the damned, Spenser's living dead cannot find release from their inner torment; thus guilt and remorse torture Redcrosse and Phedon, and despair after Daphne's death overwhelms Alcyon. Like the "bootlesse" wailings of the damned in hell (*FQ* 1.5.33), the sufferings of Spenser's living dead seem endless and without escape as "cruell death doth scorne to come at call" (*Daphnaida* 356). Besides, the Christian discourse on what life and death really are and mean, which permeates Spenser's work, makes readers aware that it is not a good death that his living dead long for. In Spenser's narratives physical death as release is not the answer; the only "death" that can release people from the "old man" within who lives the living death of the flesh, is the death of the "old man," a transformation that God's grace only can effect. The narrative of Maleger very effectively dramatizes this view, as I shall show in the next chapter.

---

[107] The Spenserian living dead look like Contemplation, but whereas the sunken eyes and hollow cheeks of the living dead are visible signs of their inner necrosis, Contemplation's "blunt and bad" eyes (1.10.47) and his great leannes (st. 48) signify his detachment from earthly and mortal concerns and the predominance in him of the spiritual over the physical.

[108] On hell conceived of as either a condition or a place, or both, in the Christian (Catholic and Protestant) tradition, see Patrides and Wittreich 186-89 and Maresca's article "Hell" in the *Spenser Encyclopedia*.

7. The Living Death of the "Old Man"

I think Spenser's emphasis on his living dead's longing for deliverance from themselves has not received the critical attention it deserves. It signals the importance in his texts of the Christian idea that people harbour corruption within themselves. Julia Kristeva has skilfully traced the shift of theological focus from the couple of antonyms "pur/impur" that is at the base of the Old Testament ethical and normative discourse, to the dichotomy "dehors/dedans" of the New Testament (*Pouvoirs de l'horreur* 135). It is a crucial shift of very great doctrinal and psychological import. No longer conceived of as something (some food, diseases, menstrual blood, etc.) external to people that pollutes or profanes them when they come into contact with it, corruption in the New Testament is seen as internal to human beings, originating from within. Sins, evils, perversions are in the human heart, abjection is in people and threatens their pure identities from within: "Retire we our selues into our selues, we finde it there as vncleane as any where" (Mornay sig. D^v).[109] Spenser's texts dramatize the psychological need to exclude what is impure, the impulse to discard one's sinful and corrupt self in order to discard corruption. As the context of the narratives makes clear, his suffering characters display a confused and in many ways perverted version of this impulse, as they long to get rid of whatever (life, conscience, feeling) brings torment. What a good Christian should long for, instead, as Spenser shows, is the death of the "old man," the living dead within who harbours corruption. One should long for the ejection of the Maleger and Despair in oneself, but that only God's love and grace can effect, not death. One should long for a purified, saved, new spiritual self to be

---

[109] Mornay's tract, *A discovrse of life and death*, which was very popular in Spenser's day especially in the Sidney circle, offers many reflections on the view that we "cary with vs our auarice, our ambition, our riotousnesse, all our corrupt affections. [. . .] Change bed, chamber, house, countrey, againe and againe: we shall euery where find the same vnrest, because euery where we finde our selues" (D2^v).

admitted to eternity after a fulfilled earthly life, not for the oblivion of an impure, conscience-burdened and embittered self in death.

From both dramatic and allegorical points of view, Maleger is the most powerful of Spenser's representations of the "old man" immured in a condition of spiritual death when "the body living, the soul is dead" (Bradford 333). Depicted as a "dead-liuing swaine" and "a ghost [. . .], whose graue-clothes were vnbound" (*FQ* 2.11.44, 20), he bodies forth the state of those who, being "of the earth, earthlie" (1 Cor. 15.47), lead a life that is really a long death. Such a life is "lothfull" (st. 46) "because chthonic and carnal," merely earthly, as the function of the earth in Maleger's narrative signals (Weatherby 348). The earth is in fact the source of Maleger's life, viz of that living death to which he is restored each time he falls on it, seemingly dead.

"As pale and wan as ashes," his skin "all withered like a dryed rooke," he wears "a dead mans skull" (2.11.22) on his head: he is the image of mortality, of "inherited death" and all it implies in terms of physical and moral corruption (Weatherby 345).[110] He lays siege to Alma's castle, an allegory of the human body, as mortality lays siege to each and every person.[111] He commands a "monstrous rablement / Of fowle misshapen wights" (st. 8), each representing a sin, a temptation, a bodily weakness, an illusory good, all that strengthens the "old man," one's "graceless self" (Maleger is "most strong in most infir-

---

[110] Weatherby argues convincingly that Maleger is to be seen more as "inherited death" than "inherited sin" as scholars like A. S. P. Woodhouse and A. C. Hamilton, whose views he summarizes and discusses at 345-46, have maintained. Weatherby makes his point through an accurate and learned exploration of the patristic view of sin and grace. As Schoenfeldt points out, Maleger can also be understood "to represent a predominant humor: his 'leane and meagre' physiognomy and his 'cold and drery' complexion denote melancholy (2.11.22)" (51). As we have seen, melancholy is the mark of the "old man."

[111] Cf. St Paul: "But I see another lawe in my members, rebelling against the lawe of my minde, and leading me captiue unto the lawe of sinne, which is in my members" (Rom. 7.23).

mitee" [st. 40]) (McCabe, *Pillars* 176).[112] "Flesh without bloud, a person without spright, / Wounds without hurt, a bodie without might": Maleger's narrative develops the view that the "old man" is a living dead, a "lifelesse shadow" (2.11.40, 44). Without the spiritual joy that is one of the gifts of regenerate life, man is a Maleger, viz, a "carkasse" with breath (st. 38).

As an embodiment of the "old man," the fleshly sinful, mortal, fallen self that in every person contends with the spiritual and regenerate self for predominance, Maleger cannot die before he is touched by Grace.[113] In fact, the three catalepses preceding his death in the "standing lake" (2.11.46), an image of baptism, do not release him from himself.[114] Each time he revives, he is unchanged, still caught in the process of decay and corruption: nothing but God's grace can make the old mortal man die and the new spiritual one take his place.

Maleger's three deaths remind me of the three deaths – from spiritual death in life, to physical death that is "the beginning of eternall death" (Perkins, *Salve* 513) – to which, as theologians incessantly warned, those incapable of changing from "old" into "new" men are doomed. Maleger's state prior to his final demise is similar to the paradoxical state of the damned who are spiritually and physically dead and yet are not granted that death that leads to life, the death of their sinful and corrupt self, the death of the "old man."

The most effective and powerfully evocative dramatization in Spenser's work of the living deadness that attends enslavement to the

---

[112] McCabe argues that Maleger is Arthur's "graceless self."

[113] Despair's unsuccessful attempts at hanging himself (1.9.54) are another dramatization of the idea that physical death cannot make the "old man" characterized by lack of spiritual joy die. Despair is a powerful figure of the state of living deadness that attends the unregenerate life; as I observed in Chapter 4 above, everything in him and around him, from appearance to dwelling, points to death and mortality.

[114] Maleger's are mock resurrections like that of Sansjoy whose narrative is discussed below. Both are restored not to life but to that death that is the life of the flesh.

"old man" is Sansjoy's mock resurrection in Book 1 of *The Faerie Queene*. Generally overlooked by Spenserian scholarship, the episode seems to me to be as crucial for the definition of the motif of living death in Spenser's work, as the narrative of Contemplation for that of the death-wish. While Contemplation's words to Redcrosse highlight the difference between godly and ungodly desires of death, the narrative of Sansjoy and Aesculapius clarifies what the inversion of the terms 'life' and 'death' really means from a spiritual perspective and thus implicitly exposes the very limited mortal apprehension of its significance that Spenser's suffering characters display when they call life a long death because of its painfulness.

Seriously wounded after his combat with Redcrosse, Sansjoy is rescued by Duessa and brought by Night to Aesculapius, the pagan healer, in "deepe *Auernus* hole" (1.5.31).[115] There he recovers a life which participates in the natures of both death and hell as it is obtained in hell at the request of Night, associated with death and one of death's images since antiquity, through Aesculapius, a damned soul who has been thrown "vnto hell [. . .] aliue" (st. 40) and who is a false image of that other Healer who has descended to hell alive.[116] The new life Sansjoy is given can be nothing but a renewal of the living death of the "old man" that is mortal life. Aesculapius cannot deliver him from the "bodie of this death" (Rom. 7.24); he cannot give Sansjoy the "joy" which is one of the gifts of the Spirit, and thus, he can only restore breath to a carcass.

The episode of Sansjoy's physical healing in hell acquires richer significance when it is considered in the light of Redcrosse's spiritual

---

[115] In his *Spenser Encyclopedia* article on "Aesculapius," Hoeniger reviews the classical sources of the myth of Jove's wrath at Aesculapius's "resurrection" of the dead Hippolytus following which the physician is thrown into hell alive. Donald Cheney in *Spenser's Image of Nature* argues that "by destroying the powers of death, he [Aesculapius] has prepared for himself an endlessly painful life against which his salves are of no avail" (51).

[116] On Aesculapius as a conventional figure of a false Christ, see A. C. Hamilton, *The Structure of Allegory* 70-71.

healing in the House of Holiness.[117] The two narratives, clearly paralleled, illustrate very well the idea, so often referred to by Spenser, of the inversion of meaning between life and death and point to the important fact that in Spenser's work life and death are constantly viewed in a double perspective, the earthly and the spiritual. All that is evil and corrupt in the first episode (the setting, the characters who take care of Sansjoy) become, in the second, holy and virtuous (Una substitutes for Duessa, the House of Holiness for hell, and Fidessa for Aesculapius). The two narratives dramatize the differences between false and true healing and reveal what true life is as distinguished from living death. Sansjoy is healed in his body only, hence what is corruptible and destined to death is preserved in him, thus preparing him to pursue mortal life, that is, his protracted death. In Redcrosse's case, physical recovery is effected by "mortifying" the body, and is just a preliminary to care of his soul, that is, of the spiritual and the incorruptible in him that will enable him to participate in godly living and eventually cross the threshold forbidden to all that is mortal and sinful. Thus whereas Sansjoy is taken care of with a view to his return to a "sansjoy" life that is really death, Redcrosse is prepared for cooperation in the providential plan and a future holy death that will be really a birth.

Like Tantalus of whom Spenser says, in the Garden of Proserpina, that he "daily dyde, yet neuer throughly dyen couth" (2.7.58), Maleger and Sansjoy are trapped in a death that no death can obliterate. Whereas Spenser's suffering characters tend to immure themselves in stasis in an effort to avoid pain and loss, Spenser here presents the absence of change as awful. It is the inability of Maleger, Tantalus and other figures of living dead like Despair, Sansjoy, and Malbecco to change that produces horror. Their stasis has nothing in common with

---

[117] Hoeniger highlights Spenser's receptivity to the medieval reading of the story of Aesculapius's restoration of life to Hippolytus as a dramatization of the difference between "spiritual healing by the divine" and "mere therapy of the body by physicians" (10).

that for which Spenser himself longs at the close of the *Mutabilitie Cantos*; their stasis is rather a paralysis of being than that final stability in God towards which change drives everything as envisioned in the *Cantos*.[118] Unable to change, to shed the mortal and sinful in them, they are walled up in a death that never changes and thus never turns into a rebirth, either a spiritual rebirth in the course of life, or an eternal rebirth at the end of it.

The narratives of abstractions such as Maleger and Sansjoy whose living death is irrevocable, imply that the fully "human," that is, the godly human, partakes in life whatever its pains and is open to change, especially to the operations of Grace. This view is skilfully dramatized in the allegory of Malbecco (*FQ* 3.9-10), which traces the degeneracy of a mortal human to an undying abstraction.

Malbecco is characterized by stasis and obsession: "all his dayes he drownes in priuitie," avoiding contact with people and involvement in virtuous action, his mind "set on mucky pelfe" (3.9.8, 4). Immured in the living death of fleshly attachment to ephemera, he forces his (as yet) innocent young wife Hellenore into the living death of a futile life of isolation and sterility far from "all mens sight, / Depriu'd of kindly ioy and naturall delight" (st. 5).

When Hellenore elopes with Paridell and a substantial portion of her husband's wealth, grief at the simultaneous loss of the human and material possessions whose guarding was his raison d'être drives Malbecco to utter despair.[119] Realization that the "God of his desire" (3.10.15), gold, and that Hellenore herself are irremediably lost, starts his metamorphosis into an abstraction, the figure of a psychic and spiritual state. A. C. Hamilton rightly argues that the "addition" in the

---

[118] Oram points to *"The Faerie Queene*'s larger concern with paralysis – with a state in which characters find themselves vulnerable and helpless to influence their condition and that of the world around them" ("Spenserian Paralysis" 51).

[119] Andrew Escobedo suggests that Malbecco experiences "a reduction of self to world – what Kierkegaard calls an excessive 'finitude' (33) – wherein we identify ourselves only with the material things before us [. . .]" (81).

II The Psychology of Despair 95

narrator's remark that Malbecco "ran away, ran with himselfe away" (st. 54), "points to the disintegration of his person" (Hamilton's 1977 edition of the *FQ* 399). Malbecco assumes the ghost-like appearance of one "from Limbo lake [. . .] late escaped" (st. 54). Significantly, the narrator explains Malbecco's unsuccessful attempted suicide when he throws himself from a hill (st. 56) by pointing out that

> [. . .] through long anguish, and selfe-murdring thought
> He was so wasted and forpined quight,
> That all his substance was consum'd to nought,
> And nothing left [. . .]. (3.10.57)

Malbecco loses his human features and turns into an "aery Spright," the essence itself of the "long anguish, and self-murdring thought" (3.10.57) that has reduced him to this sorry state.[120] He turns into a passion, here jealousy, which feeds itself "with selfe-consuming smart" (3.11.1).[121] He "is woxen so deform'd, that he has quight / Forgot he was a man, and *Gealosie* is hight" (3.10.60); Malbecco has become so identified with vice that he has lost the humanity which alone promises deliverance from mortal life. Forever trapped in a state of

---

[120] Pauline Parker argues that the more a character in Spenser slips towards the bottom of the hierarchy of being, the more he or she loses "life, substance, beauty, happiness and being" (43). The Spenserian hierarchy, in fact, "depends on degrees of being in this sense that, as we descend the scale, which is a scale of moral values, the creatures on each step become not only less good but, in virtue of that less good, less real, less substantial" (43).

[121] At 3.11.1 jealousy is described as the "vilest [. . .] of all the passions in the mind" and in *An Hymne of Loue* 267-68 the ravages of "That cancker worme" are described: "[jealousy] eates the hart, and feedes vpon the gall." In his *Spenser Encyclopedia* article "Malbecco" Skulsky rightly observes that to Spenser's eyes jealousy is the "vilest" of passions "because it debases the noblest of them" (449). Babb remarks that "in Elizabethan literature, jealousy is often characterized as a mental disease" (173).

frightful immutability, he can "neuer dye, but dying liues" (3.10.60).[122]

The risks for people's spiritual and psychological wholesomeness inherent in resistance to change arising from a fleshly and merely plaintive apprehension of the significance of life and death are a central theme in *Daphnaida*, Spenser's unconventional elegy which I shall analyse in Part III.

---

[122] A suggestive exploration of the different levels of meaning attached to the narrative of Malbecco is Berger's "The Discarding of Malbecco" in *Revisionary Play* 154-71.

III
Bereavement and Elegy

8. The Formal and Thematic Orthodoxy of "November"

My focus so far has been on Spenserian narratives which dramatize the consequences in terms of despair of fleshly views of suffering and death. I have demonstrated how the emphasis in a large number of Spenser's fictions of trials, short of bereavement, falls on the mortal weakness and vulnerability of the "old man" who sees things from an earthly perspective that renders life meaninglessly painful, and that arouses loathing of life and longing for death.

As we have seen, while these responses are often represented in Spenser's work as unsurprising and even understandable, they are never condoned. Whether implicitly or explicitly, Spenser's texts always set earthbound perspectives which arouse impatience and despair against the divine perspective of those like Contemplation. In such a perspective, toils and tribulations acquire meaning as trials of faith and as necessary steps in a path leading to life eternal through death, a door only God may open.

I now wish to demonstrate that confrontation between earthly and divine perspectives is also crucial to the Spenserian fictions of responses to bereavement. I shall argue that the eleventh eclogue of *The Shepheardes Calender* which includes an exposition of the significance of death in the light of Christian faith, and a condemnation of excessive mourning, represents ideal responses to bereavement, while *Daphnaida* represents fleshly responses and their consequences in terms of immurement in despair.

Both "November" and *Daphnaida* deal with the experience of death and mourning. Both works dramatize how, on the occasion of specific deaths, survivors move into a liminal position whence, philosophically standing "on the edge," they contemplate life from the perspective of death and death and the afterlife from the perspective of mortality. Both works dramatize also the capacity or incapacity of the bereaved to overcome dismay and despair.[123] Both "November" and *Daphnaida* are pastoral elegies, but in imagery, emphasis and mood, they could hardly differ more and it is precisely in the light of these striking contrasts that *Daphnaida* seems less "a pastoral elegy manqué," as many critics think, than a successful innovation.[124] It is my view that reading *Daphnaida* alongside "November" helps an appreciation of the rhetorical strategies Spenser employs in the later poem. The function of

---

[123] Since my present aim is to analyze the extent and significance of departures in *Daphnaida* from the formal and thematic decorums of pastoral elegy that "November" keeps, my reading of the latter necessarily rests on the literal and tropological meanings of the text that make it a dramatization of a specific death and a piece of persuasion about Christian views of mortality and mourning. However, I am aware of the anagogical and allegorical readings of the figure of Dido discussed in *Variorum* 7: 402-404, and in suggestive studies such as McLane, "Elizabeth and Dido" in *Spenser's Shepheardes Calender* and Whipp's "Weep for Dido." A convenient study of critical views is found in Berger 394-96.

[124] Oram, "Daphnaïda" 487. The number of contemptuous assessments of *Daphnaida* exceeds by far that of favourable ones. Often seen as an unsuccessful imitation of Chaucer's *Book of the Duchess*, it has occasioned some almost naïve remarks by otherwise acute critics: William Renwick sees it as an attempt "to compensate with ingenuity of craftmanship for the lack of genuine feeling" (62), C. S. Lewis defines it a "garish thing of stucco disguised as marble" (370), and William Nelson thinks it is an aborted attempt to "vary the traditional form" of the elegy (69). I think these reactions (and the many others similar to these one could quote) express a sense of unease before *Daphnaida*, or, as Martin puts it so well, "a moralistic disapproval of elegies that do not reintegrate their mourners into the mainstream of society" (83). Too often, instead of wondering why *Daphnaida* is so atypical, critics have dismissed it as an eccentric work. Only recently some Spenserians have shown that new critical approaches to *Daphnaida* yield interesting fruits. I think Oram's "*Daphnaida* and Spenser's Later Poetry" is the best treatment of *Daphnaida*. My own discussion is indebted to it, although I disagree with Oram's inclination to identify the narrator with Spenser and see the poem as a warning to a friend from one who knew by experience the risks inherent in indulging grief. When I first drafted my discussion of *Daphnaida*, I had not seen Harris and Steffen's suggestive study "The Other Side of the Garden" which anticipates some of my arguments.

Spenser's departures in *Daphnaida* from certain crucial conventions of the elegiac genre and his construction of a pastoral elegy that is really an "antipastoral" becomes also more visible.[125]

Many of Spenser's contemporary readers would have known what to expect, formally and thematically, from works belonging to the genre of pastoral elegy. The genre was highly codified, offering a repertoire of conventions such as a framework of traditional settings, imagery, figures, appropriate language and rhetorical structures.[126] Hence any departure from the conventional pattern is significant and is likely to have been noticed by contemporary readers. In Spenser's day the issue of mourning was receiving a great deal of attention from churchmen, philosophers and moralists.[127] By virtue of sermons, instructions for letters of consolation, and moral and religious tracts centring on the boundary between acceptable and censurable expressions of mourning, Spenser's readers are likely to have been aware of theological and philosophical views of orthodox responses to bereavement and might therefore easily notice any departure from them. I shall argue that *Daphnaida* relies heavily on readers' perceptions of its numerous and conspicuous breaks with the rules of literary decorum and the thematic orthodoxy to which "November" conforms.

"November" is a masterly technical performance; it is the expression, as Dennis Kay observes, of a "social exchange [. . .], the utterance of a professional commissioned to articulate the grief of a patron

---

[125] "*Daphnaida* is explicitly an antipastoral – a formal, highly structured song of grief which everywhere denies the efficacy of either song or form" (Harris and Steffen 27).

[126] On the formal and thematic conventions of the pastoral elegy, see Ellen Z. Lambert's finely researched volume *Placing Sorrow: A Study of the Pastoral Elegy Convention from Theocritus to Milton*. For a shorter treatment, see her article "Elegy, pastoral" in *The Spenser Encyclopedia* 234-35.

[127] Pigman gives an excellent account of influential early modern literary, moral and theological treatments of the issue of mourning. He argues that "Spenser's contemporaries" were "saturated [. . .] in the literature of consolation" (78). See also the informative chapter "Grief and Mourning" in Houlbrooke's *Death, Religion, and the Family*.

in terms which conform to the decorums of subject and season" (31).[128] Colin's poetic performance in "November" is to be seen in this light. Colin is one who, although already in a plaintive mood because of his love-melancholy, laments upon request someone else's loss, and therefore assumes the role of the professional elegist who is in no way emotionally involved in the loss he is singing of. Whereas in "November" the principal mourner is always behind the scenes, in *Daphnaida* he is constantly on stage and it is he who speaks the elegy. Appropriately then, the emphasis in the two elegies falls on two different objects: in "November" it is the significance of individual deaths and mortality as part of natural, human, and divine exigencies, in *Daphnaida* it is the experience of grief and despair following bereavement.

Colin sings to comply with Thenot's request and obtain from him the promised "gyfts for guerdon" ("November" 45). A representative of authors of commissioned elegies memorializing public figures or relatives and friends of patrons, he expects to be rewarded for the poetic service he offers. "Gyfts," however, are not Colin's only incentive to write verse; he is also tempted (Colin uses this verb at line 49) by the artistic challenge. Thenot urges him to prove he is no less inspired as a poet of "sorrowe and deathes dreeriment" than of love-melancholy (36, 44). Colin's plaintive mood and the context and atmosphere of the current season, "sadde Winter" (13), complement his inspiration. But Colin's main help towards making his song successful, viz towards making it a valuable piece of poetry that instructs and consoles mourners, is literary precedent. Thenot exhorts Colin to follow in the footsteps of "hem, that learned bee, / And han be watered at the Muses well" (29-30). "November" belongs in the genre of the classical pastoral eclogue, whose greatest and most influential examples are Theocritus's *Idyll*, Bion's *Lament for Adonis*, Moschus's *Lament for Bion* and Virgil's fifth *Eclogue*. These eclogues set the pat-

---

[128] In the letter to Gabriel Harvey prefaced to the *Shepheardes Calender*, E. K. praises Spenser's "dewe obseruing of Decorum euerye where, in personages, in seasons, in matter, in speach."

tern, especially as regards structure, imagery and argument, which elegists through the classical as well as Renaissance periods either followed faithfully or kept as a point of departure for their experiments. John Hankins has argued convincingly that the archetypal model for "November," which E. K. describes in the argument as an elegy "made in imitation" of Marot's *Complainct de Madame Loyse de Savoie* (1531), is Moschus's *Lament for Bion*.[129] Indeed, "November" shares a number of images and arguments with the *Lament*, whose ascensional movement from registration of facts, through description of grief, remembrance of happier days, melancholy meditation upon universal mortality, to final acceptance and consolation, it reproduces closely.

In "November" Spenser builds his argument and shapes his poetry according to the pattern in five stages which was the mark of elegies of a traditional kind and which Julius Caesar Scaliger, a widely read authority in Spenser's day, described as a well-balanced succession of "praise, demonstration of loss, lament, consolation, and exhortation" (qtd. in Pigman 42).[130] The harmonious structure wherein proportioned space is assigned to each stage provides the framework through which "November" aspires to what Harris and Steffen call the highest end of elegy which is "to order and exorcise that most ineffable and universal of human experiences: loss" (19).

If "November" complies with most of the formal and rhetorical conventions of classical pastoral elegy, its ideology is unmistakably Christian. The Christian theme is introduced in the poetically powerful turn from the mournful tone of lines 60-162 marked by the refrains "O heauie herse," "O carefull verse," to lines 165-69 where Dido's apotheosis is first referred to and the refrains are modified into "O happye

---

[129] Hankins argues that "in the manner in which it represents phases of grief, ["November" is the first elegy] in English to follow the Greek pastoral model, as illustrated by the lament of Moschus for Bion" (*Variorum* 7: 397).

[130] Pigman quotes the crucial passages from Julius Caesar Scaliger's *Poetices Libri Septem* and describes its author as "the most influential Renaissance author of poetics" (42).

herse," "O ioyfull verse" (from line 170). The Christian theme is prepared for by a survey of the various phases of grief which heal mourners. This crucial itinerary is absent from *Daphnaida*; instead of going through stages of grief, Alcyon is immured in the initial phase of the healing process, that of despair. A careful analysis of such itinerary in "November" will be useful for my discussion of the later elegy.

In the first stanza of the elegy proper (which starts at line 53) two ideas, those of sadness and stillness, are suggested in connection with death, as Melpomene, the "mournefulst Muse" (53), is urged to supply inspiration for a song about the fact that Dido is dead and "lyeth wrapt in lead" (59). In the second stanza, shepherds, encouraged to bewail Dido, are said to be bereft of her "light," to "dwell in deadly night" (68, 69). It is a time of dismay, when melancholy suffocates other feelings and vital impulses (at line 71 the shepherds cease piping). Stanza three introduces the theme of melancholy reflection on human subjection to mortality; death seems to have triumphed over Dido who must "into dust ygoe" (76), and over her survivors "whose better dayes death hath shut vp in woe" (74). The fourth stanza supplies new ground for pessimism in its reference to the fact that whereas the "flouret of the field" fades and "lyeth buryed" in winter only to revive in spring (83, 84), when human beings die, they "reliuen not" (89). A practised reader used to detecting implied discourses and to Christian conventions of elegy may well regard this reflection upon the extraneousness of human beings from the natural cycle of life, death, and regeneration as a preparation for the Christian theme of resurrection and death's final defeat. People's exclusion from the circular process of death and rebirth that characterizes the natural life-cycle points out a different destiny for them. The sixteenth-century reader accustomed to arguing by analogy and implication might well see in the difference between human and vegetable regeneration an implied allusion to the immortality of the soul.[131]

The dirge proceeds to cover the traditional stages of eulogy of the dead (st. 5) and exposition of the effect of this death on the principal mourner, Lobbinol, and on the natural world that seems to join in the mourning (sts. 6-10). Stanzas 6-10 represent manifestations of intense sorrow as necessary elements of the healing process, since the final phase of the elegy which leads to acceptance and consolation starts only when extremes of grief are fully spent.[132] Stanza 11 develops the view that despair is at least partly overcome when, to use Harry Berger's formulation, the contingent loss is seen in the light of Loss.[133] Viewed in a larger perspective that embraces the human condition in general, the particular tragedy of Dido's death is a reminder of the fact that mortality and the misery attendant on it, are a common heritage. Dido is now mourned less as an individual, than as a symbol of human frailty and mortality.

At this point Colin's song dramatizes the view that since the "state of earthly things [is] trustlesse" (153), people should not get too attached to them. This melancholy meditation paves the way for the introduction in stanza 12 of the theme of hope and consolation. If "nys on earth assuraunce to be sought" (157), then it is to be sought elsewhere, if not on earth, then in heaven. Faith in resurrection, "Dido nis dead, but into heauen hent" (169), is the only effective consolation to human dismay at the ravages of mutability and mortality. Suffering is presented as unavoidable, given that the path leading to heaven traverses the earth where people "swincke and sweate for nought" (154),

---

[131] I would not agree with Harry Berger's inference in *Revisionary Play* 407 that failure of the "consoling model of natural process [. . .] to accomodate human death in general" is an expression of "radical pessimism."

[132] In the penultimate line of his elegy for Dido, Colin says: "Ceasse now my song, my woe now wasted is" ("November" 201).

[133] Berger argues that "the Muses' *November* gift to Colin thus consists of elegiac conventions enabling the singer to redirect attention from death to loss and from loss to Loss" (406).

but it is a temporary experience that Christians should face patiently, with the eternity of "blisse" (194) awaiting them always in view. Stanza twelve finally dramatizes Dido's apotheosis. She has broken the "bonds [. . .] of eternall night" to go and live "with the blessed Gods in blisse" (165, 194). If her death reminds survivors of their mortality, her resurrection reminds them they are equally destined to life eternal; Dido, in fact, is "gone afore (whose turne shall be the next?)" (193). But belief in Dido's triumph over death through resurrection makes mourning problematic now.

Stanzas 12-14 reproduce contemporary condemnations of what were held to be expressions of ungodly and excessive mourning. As we have seen, in Spenser's day, moral philosophers and theologians meditated upon "the moral problem of grief," discussed where to draw the line between rational and irrational, godly and ungodly, expressions of mourning and warned the bereaved that immoderate grief was a sign of "irrationality, weakness, inadequate self-control, and impiety" (Pigman 75, 2).[134] The issue is crucial for discussions of "November" and *Daphnaida*; one of the more remarkable and significant differences between the two elegies, in fact, is that the first proposes an orthodox model of behaviour in bereavement, while the second drama-

---

[134] On expressions of grief as symptomatic of the mourner's impiety, irrationality and lack of self-control, and therefore the object of harsh condemnation from the most influential sixteenth-century moralists and theologians, see Pigman, esp. Chapter 1. See also Houlbrooke, *Death, Religion, and the Family* 220-23 and 253. Besides theology, physiology (physicians regarded immoderate grief as a disease endangering physical and mental health, see Babb 103-05) and classical philosophy (passages from Seneca's *Letters to Lucilius* and Cicero's *Tusculan Questions* on the irrationality of falling prey to despair following a natural event like the death of loved ones were very often quoted) supplied arguments to critics of excessive mourning. In "Against Sorrow for Death of Friends or otherwise" in his *Anatomy of Melancholy*, Burton surveys religious, philosophical and medical treatments of the issue and says that "howsoever this passion of sorrow be violent, bitter, and seizeth familiarly on wise, valiant, discreet men, yet it may surely be withstood, it may bee diverted" (memb.5, subsec. 1; 2: 176-186).

tizes in Alcyon an attitude that would have horrified moralists and churchmen.

"November" develops the view that while expressions of dismay and inconsolable sorrow are acceptable and even beneficial in the initial phases of mourning, their persistence when the bereaved is calm enough to consider the fate of the dead, is a sign of irrationality and impiety. Colin presents the continuing mourning of the bereaved as both ungodly and irrational by challenging those who grieve after his metaphoric description of Dido's resurrection: since "she hath the bonds broke of eternall night," "why then weepes Lobbin so without remorse?" (165, 167). Reflecting once again on the deceased's happy state, "Dido nis dead, but into heauen hent" (169), Colin realizes the general climate of sadness and mourning is inappropriate, hence his tirade against the attitude of all those present, including himself: "Why wayle we then? why weary we the Gods with playnts, / As if some euill were to her betight?" (173-74). This is nearly a poetic replica word by word, concept by concept, of some of the arguments proposed by those who argued with most intensity in the years of Spenser's literary career for the moderation and even suppression of grief in mourning which the most influential moralists and preachers considered as unworthy of both the wise man and the true Christian.[135] Erasmus, who is probably the harshest Renaissance critic of mourning, asks a question which is similar to Colin's: if we really believe our dead are among the blessed, why do we "mourne and weepe"? ("A treatise" Riii^v). Along the same lines, Thomas Becon has his sick man deplore his neighbours' declared intention to mourn his loss; Epaphroditus first highlights the irrationality of their weeping for him, "Why for me? Because good things haue chaunced vnto me?" then openly

---

[135] Spenser's narratives of bereavement never advocate suppression of grief. In "November," as in the fictions of Una and Calidore's supposed bereavements which I discuss later, even extreme manifestations of dismay and despair are represented sympathetically as necessary preliminaries to acceptance of loss and consolation. In *Daphnaida* what is censured is not the intensity of Alcyon's grief but its chronic persistence.

refers to the impiety of mourning in general "Let the heathen, which have no hope of the joyful immortality of the soul [. . .] mourn, weep, and lament for their deceased" (*Sicke Mannes Salue* 120, 124).[136]

If stanzas 12 and 13 of "November" dramatize orthodox attitudes to mourning, stanza 14 quite unsurprisingly offers the only other expression in Spenser's work besides that found in the episode of Redcrosse's instruction on the Mount of Contemplation (*FQ* 1.10) of what contemporary theology would view as a godly desire of death. Stanzas 13 and 14 represent death as desirable mainly because it gives access to heaven. Even the strictest theologian would approve of the kind of longing for death Colin expresses; when he affirms he longs to be with Dido in "*Elisian* fieldes" (179), "Might I once come to thee" (181), it is clear his wish does not arise from loathing of this life, but from a godly yearning for the next. Colin seems to repeat Calvin's statement that if Christians reflected on death's gift to them, they would "burn with the zeal for death" (1: 716), in Colin's words "dye would we dayly, once it to expert [i.e. experience]" (186).

Introducing a theme which recurs in other Spenserian narratives of bereavement, stanza 15 dramatizes the survivors' sense that the condition of the dead is far happier than their own.[137] The "there" of Dido's abode and the "here" (194, 199) of the survivors' stand in marked opposition; "there" she "ioyes enioyes, that mortall men doe misse" (196). Dido's gain through death is immense; while "here on earth"

---

[136] Cf. Myles Coverdale: "The heathen and unbelievers mourn without hope of the resurrection" (122). The fact that Coverdale devotes as many as seven chapters (1-4 and 6-8) of his "Treatise on Death" to exhortations to moderate mourning, "unmeasurable sorrow and heaviness" (120), is a sign of the contemporary concern with the issue.

[137] See my discussion of these narratives in Chapter 9 of the present study. As I will demonstrate, while in "November" Dido's condition is envied by survivors mainly because of the celestial bliss she enjoys, elsewhere in Spenser's work his bereaved characters express their sense that the dead are happier mainly because they are spared life's miseries. Whereas in "November" the emphasis is on the condition of the dead, everywhere else it falls on that of the living.

she was just "poore shepheards pryde," she now is "the honor [. . .] of highest gods" (199, 198, 197). In this light, further mourning for Dido would seem impious and irrational.

"November" dramatizes contemporary views of rational, godly and healing responses to bereavement. There is a time to "weepe" when the bereaved give vent to their grief and thus enter the healing process that culminates in their recovering balance and self-command, and a time to "reioyce" (205) in consideration of the deceased's bliss and in anticipation of one's own resurrection. In this light, *"la mort ny mord,"* as the "November" emblem says; death is "the grene path way to lyfe" (E. K.'s *glosse*) and not a "doome of ill desert" (184) as "vnwise and wretched men" who cannot "weete whats good or ill" (183) think.[138] The last stage in the healing process that "November" dramatizes is reintegration into life. Thenot, who had asked Colin to "bewayle [his] wofull tene" (41), has been consoled and is ready to go back to active life, to resume his duty, as his exhortation to Colin to join him on his way back home where both will take up again their pastoral tasks signifies (207-08).

As Colin gets his "cossette" (206), it is clear that his poetic performance should be judged successful and considered to have attained the aim of pastoral elegies which is "to order and exorcise [. . .] loss" (Harris and Steffen 19).[139] In this light, "November" is a demonstration of the consolatory power traditionally ascribed to those elegies

---

[138] Berger argues that the emblem "bears a double significance in the context of the elegy: it emphasizes that this is not so much personal expression as poetic exercise or experiment, and it reminds us that in recreative metamorphosis death has no bite because life has disappeared into art" (401). These suggestions fit well into Berger's reading of "November" as a poem focusing less on death than on "rymes" (400), but I think the openly Christian framework of E. K.'s gloss should not be overlooked.

[139] Commenting on the "elegiac movement from 'heavie herse' to 'happy herse' and 'carefull verse' to 'joyfull verse,'" Berger observes that "the birth of verse is the burial of death and the death of grief" (401). More generally, Julia Kristeva points out that the healing process begins when loss is transferred or translated into language (*Soleil noir* 53).

whose structure and argument conform to conventional patterns. More generally, "November" affirms the instructive and transfiguring powers of poetry.

9. *Daphnaida*: An Unconventional Elegy

While "November" concludes with an orthodox statement of contemporary theological and philosophical views of how the wise Christian should behave when bereaved and more generally when facing the facts of mutability and mortality, *Daphnaida* is an anthology of wrong attitudes and responses. "November" represents recognition that in the perspective of faith everything, even tragedy, is endowed with meaning, as a bulwark against despair. It dramatizes the view that patience, courage and hope are gained or regained when things are seen through the eye of the spirit. It can be argued that *Daphnaida* develops the same view but only by implication, through its representation of fleshly views of life and death as a source of delusion and despair. My contention is that limited perspectives that show one face of the coin only are the subject of *Daphnaida*. Indeed, the fact of Lady Douglas Howard's death soon moves backstage and the wary reader realizes this atypical but carefully constructed elegy is written neither to praise and memorialize the dead, nor to console survivors.[140] The emphasis is on responses to bereavement and more generally to the facts of life and death arising from earthly perspectives within which only half of the whole picture is visible. Unlike traditional elegies, *Daphnaida* seems aimed less at making the living accept the fact of a specific

---

[140] Oram, "*Daphnaida* and Spenser's Later Poetry" 150-51, argues convincingly that the elegy does not arise from a sense of obligation towards a patron. What patron, in fact, would appreciate such an unpleasant portrait of himself? Besides, as Oram points out, on the basis of what is known about Spenser and Gorges's biographies, Gorges was "not in a position to become Spenser's patron" (151). Indeed, *Daphnaida* functions a lot better as a work of persuasion written on the occasion of a friend's bereavement, although, as Elizabeth Heale pointed out to me, it might have been written for or at the instigation of the dedicatee, the Marquess of Northampton, Arthur Gorges's aunt, for reasons unknown to us.

death and the fact of mortality in general, than at persuading them to overcome their loathing of life and attraction to death.[141]

As I suggested earlier, *Daphnaida* calls upon the reader's ability to detect the significance of its major departures from literary and thematic decorum. Indeed, I argue that the effect on readers, used to the orthodox consolatory topics of reversals of expectations, accounts for much of the persuasive design of the poem.

Daphnaida's readers might have been familiar with Spenser's previous essay in pastoral elegy, the November eclogue of the *Calender*, which had shown he could write innovative poetry that conformed to formal and thematic decorums. Readers of "November" would not fail to notice that the same poet who had created a well-balanced elegy which illustrates the efficacy of conventional form and Christian consolation in transfiguring loss and comforting mourners, had now composed an unconventionally structured elegy which is disturbing in its monotony of theme and mood and which denies the elegiac mode's efficacy in "ordering and exorcising loss."[142]

Spenser's designs on readers may be detected from the start when they are asked to perceive the irony and implied criticism of his narrator's apparently solemn address to them. The first fourteen lines enact a sort of screening of the readership aimed at selecting the ideal audience for the elegy. This device of selecting the audience has the effect of leading readers to shift their focus from the poem and its subject to themselves, as they are asked to reflect on their present mood and, more generally, their attitude to life. The reader addressed is "What euer man he be, whose heauie mynd / [is] with griefe of mournefull great mishap opprest" (1-2). In consideration of their present or past experiences, most readers would have no problem identifying them-

---

[141] As I suggested in the introduction and argued in the chapters on death-wish and living death, Spenser's work recurrently represents characters who view life and not death as the painful and frightening thing to face.

[142] I paraphrase Harris and Steffen's longer definition of the function of traditional elegies (19).

III Bereavement and Elegy 111

selves with one who, facing a great woe, goes through a phase of emotional and psychological unbalance, his heart "opprest," his mind "heauie." Things change, however, when the narrator completes the portrait of the ideal reader of *Daphnaida* by adding that it should be one who looks for "fit matter for his cares increase" (3).[143] Spenser's readers, immersed as they were in warnings about the ungodliness of wilfully swimming in the "*Balneum Diaboli*" of melancholy and exhortations to self-mastery and suppression of extremes of passion, might be expected to detect the critique implied in line 3 (Burton 3: 411).[144]

If the reader invoked at the beginning of *Daphnaida* is the object of implicit censure, those who are banned are also the target of irony. One does feel more than a hint of scorn in the portrait of the hedonist excluded from *Daphnaida*'s readership: "who so else in pleasure findeth sense, / Or in this wretched life dooth take delight, / Let him be banisht farre away from hence" (8-10). Given that life is "wretched" (the poet as a good Protestant presents this as a fact), one who "dooth take delight" in it undoubtedly displays a good deal of irrationality or voluntary blindness. Both attitudes, that of the obsessive melancholy and that of hedonism are inappropriate in the context of orthodox advice on mourning. The text implies, I suggest, that appropriate attitudes are the product of perspectives that include the whole picture, the dark and bright sides, offering reasons for both grief and consola-

---

[143] Kristeva argues that melancholy people tend to install the lost object within themselves and thus deepen the sorrow arising from loss instead of keeping it away from themselves (*Soleil noir* 177). Other Spenserian texts besides *Daphnaida* represent sufferers who display a desire to grieve. In the August eclogue of the *Calender* Cuddie says: "Let [. . .] all that may augment / My doole, drawe neare" (164-65). It will be noticed that Alcyon's monologue borrows imagery and arguments from Cuddie's melodramatic tirade (especially from lines 151 to 189).

[144] Since he thinks it is easier for the devil to delude people when excesses of melancholy in the blood alter their imaginative and rational faculties, Burton refers to the melancholy humour as "*Balneum Diaboli*, the Divels bath."

tion. These are precisely the perspectives that the *Book of the Duchess*, Spenser's model for *Daphnaida*, dramatizes.[145] Chaucer's dream-vision offers recognition of the coexistence of life and death, renovation and decay, joy and sorrow, as a remedy for the narrator's melancholy and the mourner's despair. *Daphnaida* departs from its model in its strategy, as it dramatizes perspectives which encompass just half of the picture.[146]

Having invoked the type of the obsessive griever as *Daphnaida*'s ostensible reader, the narrator adds a qualification that illuminates the rhetorical architecture of the poem. He declares there is no room among the poem's readers for those who expect to be offered a well-shaped, traditional pastoral elegy expressing a grief that is soon subdued and transfigured into hope. He announces that in *Daphnaida* "no tunes, saue sobs and grones shall ring" (14): no Colin's dirge, then, no verses expressing "doolful pleasaunce" (*Shepheardes Calender*, "November" 204). The reader will be offered no "tunes," just an exposition in rhyme of an incurable and unrestrained consuming grief. The narrator explicitly says that *Daphnaida* is meant neither to please, nor to console; it is clearly written with concerns in mind other than the mourners' recovery. Nor is it written as a challenging opportunity for the author to display his talent and mastery of the genre (the Muses are banished at line 11) and get a reward from his client.[147] Readers at this

---

[145] See Helen Phillips, "Structure and Consolation in the *Book of the Duchess.*" Footnotes in Harris and Steffen's article provide references to studies of *The Book of the Duchess*.

[146] With regard to the influence of Chaucer's *Book of the Duchess* on *Daphnaida*, Harris and Steffen rightly point out that differences in "method and effect, substance and structure" are more significant than analogies (18). On the relationship between the two elegies, see also Oram, "*Daphnaida* and Spenser's Later Poetry," and Martin, "Spenser, Chaucer, and the Rhetoric of Elegy."

[147] Whereas Colin, in keeping with elegiac formality, invokes Melpomene, the Muse of Tragedy ("November" 53), *Daphnaida*'s narrator urges the "three fatall Sisters," the Parcae, to "approach" (16, 19). I think some remarks made by Lyons regarding Marston's collection of satires *The Scourge of Vil-*

III Bereavement and Elegy 113

point are once again led to reflect on themselves and their attitudes: what would their desire to read an elegy that declaredly lacks formal appeal and healing power signal?

Having given the game away by presenting *Daphnaida* as a carefully constructed text addressed to people immured in self-pleasing melancholy that limits and distorts their views, Spenser's narrator introduces Alcyon, an hyperbolic and at times almost caricatured representation of what they might become if they fail to correct their attitudes and perspectives. But before Alcyon moves centre stage, something crucial happens: having discussed potential readers' moods and attitudes, the narrator offers his own for their scrutiny.

When he first spots Alcyon, the narrator is immersed in a "troublous thought" (29), an obsessive thought, as the confession that it "dayly [. . .] possesse[s] [his] weaker wit" signals (30). His daily meditation upon "this worlds vainnesse and lifes wretchednesse" disturbs him, his "soule it deepely doth empassion" (34, 35). He focuses attention particularly on "the miserie / In which men liue," a misery in which he has a large share, as he declares he is "of many most, / Most miserable man" (36-38).

"As I muzed" (36), "I did espie" (38): the contemporaneousness of the narrator's absorption in melancholy and grief, and Alcyon's appearance is not casual. G. W. Pigman argues that Alcyon is "almost a fantasy in the flesh" (76), an embodiment of the narrator's "troublous" thoughts (*Daphnaida* 29). I believe Alcyon here is more than that and

---

lainy, can be profitably applied also to *Daphnaida*. She argues that the "melancholy or mad pose [. . .] justifies certain stylistic features [and] disharmonies, [. . .] or what Marston refers to as his 'yerking style'" (65). In the proem to the second book of his satires, Marston announces that "no flowery 'poetic' phrases [. . .] will adorn his poems" (Lyons 65): this is the equivalent of Spenser's "here no tunes [. . .] shall ring" (14), a very appropriate proem to a text that makes the behaviour of certain readers, of the narrator (in its initial phase) and of Alcyon/Gorges an object of irony and even satire at times. In a sense, the flaws that many commentators attribute to *Daphnaida* appear from the start as an essential part of the poem's very strategy.

the function of his appearance more complex. In the light of *Daphnaida*'s instructional framework that the introductory stanzas announce, Alcyon functions as a living warning to the narrator, and hence to those readers who display the same mood and attitude, against self-pity and excessive indulgence in melancholy thoughts. Described by the narrator as a ghastly and distracted person (lines 39-49), Alcyon bodies forth the consequences in terms of despair, degeneration, and psychological imbalance, of a false response to life and death. As his narrative shows, these responses are only partly to be imputed to an imbalance in humours, as most of the time they arise either from consideration of just half of the picture, or a jaundiced view of the whole picture through the eye of the flesh. The narrator, as I shall shortly demonstrate, learns his lesson very quickly. Confronted with the projection of what he himself might become, his concern for Alcyon and efforts at making him shake off his moral, emotional and spiritual torpor lead him to overcome self-centredness and fixation with melancholy brooding. Initially sharing the mood of *Daphnaida*'s putative readers, the narrator shows them how such weakness can be overcome and their views enlarged. Although overlooked by commentators of the poem, the narrator is really a keystone in *Daphnaida*'s persuasive architecture.

Alcyon's appearance is similar to that of other Spenserian examples of despair, especially Timias.[148] It signals that he is beside himself, deranged. Described by the narrator as a "sory wight" and "some wight forlorne" (39, 45) who sighs and groans incessantly as he walks towards him, Alcyon is "clad all in black," "his carelesse lockes,

---

[148] See my discussion in Chapter 5 above. In *Daphnaida*, as in the narratives of Redcrosse and Timias, Spenser employs the device of misrecognition by friends (at line 57 the narrator is "halfe in doubt" about Alcyon's identity) to point to the fact that despair, estrangement, and alienation, are dehumanizing factors. Significantly, as Oram points out, Alcyon looks like Despair ("*Daphnaida* and Spenser's Later Poetry" 143).

III Bereavement and Elegy 115

vncombed and vnshorne, / [his] beard all ouer growne" (40, 43-44).[149] The fact that his hair "hong long adowne" (44) is an important detail, as it suggests that his estrangement from society and carelessness for anything but his own grief are long-standing attitudes signalling his self-absorption and chronic immurement in despair. Spenser's text censures Alcyon's stasis, his being wilfully trapped (at line 378 he declares: "So will I wilfully increase my paine") in that phase of mourning that is characterized by outbursts of unrestrained grief, a phase that in "November" is temporary and a prelude to acceptance and consolation. The very name of this chronic and obsessive griever suggests that instead of overcoming grief, he is overcome by it. Alcyon, in fact, is the masculine equivalent of Alcione who, in the version of the Ovidian myth Chaucer prefaces to the *Book of the Duchess*, dies of grief when she learns her husband Seys has died.[150] Like Alcione, Alcyon is an unsuccessful mourner and, more generally, a type of those who let passion overwhelm them.

Besides utter lack of self-mastery and a morbid desire to grieve, Alcyon's response to bereavement signals also his self-centredness. His

---

[149] Appearance and behaviour make Alcyon a figure of the malcontent, the social type of the melancholic, whom Babb describes as "usually black-suited and disheveled, unsociable, asperous, morosely meditative, taciturn yet prone to occasional railing" (75). With his declared hatred of the world (lines 393-434), morbid desire to grieve (372-78), and estrangement from society (484-97), Alcyon provides a parallel for one of the more popular melancholy characters in English literature, the Jaques of Shakespeare's *As You Like It* who "hates 'th'infected world' (II, vii, 60), [and] nurses his melancholy, apparently finding great pleasure in it (II, v)" (Babb 92).

[150] As Oram points out, "Alcyon's extremity is heralded in his name" ("Daphnaïda" 208). In his edition of Spenser's *Shorter Poems* Richard McCabe remarks that "Spenser's transference of a female name to his male protagonist may be intended to suggest the emasculating effects of excessive grief – a common Renaissance topos" (643). Cf. for instance Cicero's statement in *Tusculan Questions*, a very influential work in the Renaissance, that "sorrow itself is moderated, we see, when we hold up to the mourner *the imbecility of an effeminate mind*, and praise the constancy and gravity of those who calmly resign themselves to human events" (231; emphasis mine).

attention and preoccupations are focused mainly on himself; his first reference to Daphne's premature death is at line 155 of a monologue that starts at 85.[151] Until then, Alcyon is busy lamenting his own sad situation, trying to prove his grief is more intense than that of any other griever, thinking back to the past in regret at what he has lost. Significantly, his telling of the happy time with Daphne and of her death is marked by a number of first person possessive and personal pronouns that seem excessive even in an account in the first person. The reiteration of "I," "my," "mine," "me" in his first monologue signals Alcyon's fixation with himself. In this light, he considers Daphne's death for what it takes away from him in terms of happiness and brings him in terms of grief.

Other Spenserian narratives dramatize responses to bereavement that are similar to that of Alcyon. The Spenserian bereaved tend very soon to turn their attention away from the dead to focus it on themselves. The specific loss and the woe arising from it stimulate broader reflections on the series of losses that is life in Spenser's work and the sway of mortality over all that is living. Hence the bereaved tend to muse on their own lot as mortals in a fallen world marked by mutability and decay. As their awareness of the shortcomings of life sharpens, they express the view that the fate of the dead as compared to theirs is happier. Thus Alcyon deems death a blessing, a sign of God's benevolence, and the continuance of life a curse, a sign of God's wrath: "The good and righteous he away doth take, / To plague th'vnrighteous which aliue remaine" (358-59). Lamenting Sidney's death, Verlame contrasts his present "happines" with her own situation of one "distressed" and oppressed with "mortall cares, and cumbrous worlds anoy" (*Ruines of Time* 304-06). The "there" of Sidney's heavenly bliss and the "here" (304) of the survivors' living hell are as distant one from the other as the two adverbs are close, significantly juxtaposed in

---

[151] Alcyon's reference to himself as "one that for himselfe cares nought" (93) is fraught with ironies; on the one hand he is self-absorbed, on the other hand, he is careless of his true, viz spiritual, good.

one line.[152] In the same vein, Cymoent declares she envies the fate of Marinell, her son, whom she believes has just died: "Farre better I it deeme to die with speed, / Then waste in woe and wailefull miserie" (*FQ* 3.4.38). The person who dies, she says, has to bear only one moment of intense pain when passing away, while the survivor's suffering never ends as he or she "is left to waile" his or her own "losse," therefore "life is losse, and death felicitie. / Sad life worse then glad death" (3.4.38). The bereaved in Spenser's work, then, are often portrayed weeping over their own grief more than over the dead. It is not death the ravisher of their loved ones that the bereaved lament, but the absence of death in their own lives. As I argued in my discussion of the Spenserian narratives of the death-wish and living death in Part II of the present study, the emphasis in Spenser's work falls on his characters' apprehension of life and not death as horrible and frightful.

As we have seen, Alcyon's account of his life with Daphne and her death signals his self-centredness and self-absorption which emerge more clearly still when his attitudes are set against those of the narrator. Comparison between Alcyon and the narrator and their responses to suffering is significant because both are portrayed as being oppressed by equally intense grief.[153] In fact, the narrator introduces himself to Alcyon as one "whom like wofulnesse impressed deepe, / Hath made fit mate," one who has "like cause [. . .] to waile and weepe" (64-65; 66).[154] No imperturbable Stoic, the narrator can function as a model for any ordinary, passionate person facing loss.

---

[152] The same device is used again at line 602 where the narrator compares the "there" of Sidney's "ioy" with the "here" of his own "sorrow." The adverbs "there" and "here" are juxtaposed in the same way and to the same end in "November," lines 194 and 199. See my comment in Chapter 8 above.

[153] Oram assumes that Spenser may have projected onto the narrator his own condition of bereaved husband ("Daphnaïda" 209). This is necessarily pure speculation, since the date of Machabyas Childe's death is not known.

[154] I disagree with Harris and Steffen's assumption that the narrator is capable of moving outside himself because he "has less to grieve about" (35). If this were true, the narrator's role within the instructional framework of *Daph-*

When as a "most miserable" (38) grieving person he meets the despairing Alcyon, the narrator switches his attention from his own situation to that of Alcyon. Heedless of the hostile reception his display of sympathy receives, the narrator urges Alcyon to unburden his heart by committing his story to a "trustie eare" (69), weeps when he is told about Daphne's death (171), declares that Alcyon's "plight" (170) "breeds almost equall paine" in his heart (175), tries to "comfort" and "recomfort" him as well as he can (190, 546), and even offers him hospitality (558). Here as elsewhere in Spenser's work sympathy is represented as a virtuous attitude, a sign of one's love for others and mastery over natural inclinations to self-centredness and self-absorption. The narrator's emotional response to Alcyon's suffering signals his compassion (in the meaning of the Latin word *compassio* 'shared suffering'). Whereas Stoic philosophers whose advice was highly esteemed in the sixteenth century insisted that in order to avoid being infected by passion the truly wise man should offer help to grievers, but should neither let their grief upset him, nor suffer with them, Spenser's texts (both *Daphnaida* and a number of narratives in *The Faerie Queene*) dramatize the responses of highly sympathetic characters ready to expose themselves to infection.[155]

The Spenserian "anti-Stoic" characters par excellence are Guyon, Britomart and Arthur.[156] When in Book 2, canto 1 of *The Faerie Queene* Guyon hears the dying speech of the suicide Amavia, he is deeply upset, trembles, almost faints and then tells her he is ready to "die with [her] in sorrow" if he cannot "compasse [her] reliefe" (2.1.48). Similarly, at 3.11.18 Britomart tells Scudamour that since she

---

naida would be far less significant. I think the expressions "*like* wofulnesse," "*like* cause," and "griefe findes some ease by him that *like* does beare" (64, 66, 67; emphases mine) are unambiguous evidence of the fact that Alcyon's and the narrator's woes are represented as equally intense.

[155] "For, *to pity*, to envy, to exult, to rejoice, all these the Greeks call diseases, as motions of the mind refusing obedience to reason" (Cicero 138; emphasis mine).

[156] The narrator of *The Faerie Queene* is also often sympathetic.

III Bereavement and Elegy 119

is as distressed as he is about his lady's captivity in Busirane's house, she "will with proofe of last extremity, / Deliuer her fro thence, or with her for [him] dy." Another narrative of *The Faerie Queene* openly represents grief as something that is transmitted from sufferer to reliever: in Book 1, canto 7, Arthur tells the despairing Una who thinks Redcrosse has died, "your griefe is wondrous great; / For wondrous great griefe groneth in my spright" (st. 40). By establishing a parallelism between Una's and Arthur's grief, the antimetabole, viz the repetition of the same adjective and adverb in reverse order, used by Spenser in the two clauses clearly suggests Arthur's perfect compassion; Arthur is "infected" by a perturbation as intense as Una's.

However compassionate and sympathetic, Sir Guyon, Britomart, Arthur and *Daphnaida*'s narrator nevertheless champion different responses to life and death from those of the despairing persons they try to help.[157] The juxtaposition of approaches renders evident the implied criticism of responses that arise from fleshly views of things (as in the case of Amavia, Scudamour and Alcyon), or from momentary collapse (as in the case of Una whose "bereavement" I discuss in detail later). This persuasive strategy is probably more manifest in *Daphnaida* with its articulated comparison between the attitudes of Alcyon and those of the narrator than anywhere else in Spenser's work.

The text's emphasis on the similarities between the humoral temperament, mood and situation of Alcyon and those of the narrator authorizes consideration of the two as making up one character with two faces. Afflicted by "like wofulnesse," sharing a natural inclination to melancholy and "like cause" "to waile and weepe" (64, 66), Alcyon and the narrator figure forth the type of the melancholic faced with loss. *Daphnaida* develops the view that responses depend more on one's perspective than on one's temperament or the kind of trial one faces. In *Daphnaida* two responses ascribable to two different per-

---

[157] As Harris and Steffen put it so well: in *Daphnaida*, as elsewhere in Spenser's work, the reader feels a "tension between instruction and pity" (35).

spectives are juxtaposed: the first is the transcendence of personal grief in a movement of sympathy and charity, in recognition of the fact that suffering, being part of the common lot of fallen humans, is neither exceptional nor unique; the other is immurement in despair and self-pity, an attitude that arises from the idea of having been personally wronged and a sense of the uniqueness of one's condition as sufferer. Within the Christian framework of Spenser's poetry, a view of suffering as the common destiny of human beings signals recognition of the fact of fallenness which at the same time accounts for the painfulness of the human condition and points to God's promise of redemption and exchange of eternal bliss for temporary tribulations.

As we have seen, a view of oneself as the favourite target of life's blows and of one's own loss and grief as unique, and a sense of the impossibility of finding fit words to describe an almost unspeakable grief or of being understood, often characterize the narratives of despairing sufferers in *The Faerie Queene*. However, through reiteration of the universality of the experience of loss, Spenser's texts represent such a self-centred view as fallacious and its effects, self-pity and immurement in despair, as censurable. This rhetorical strategy is supplemented in *Daphnaida* through juxtaposition of the narrator's and Alcyon's perceptions of themselves as sufferers. The narrator, aware that he shares a common lot and that given "the miserie / In which men liue," his present tribulations are neither unexpected nor unique, presents himself as of "many," not of all, "most, / Most miserable man" (36-38). Alcyon on the other hand describes himself as "the wretchedst man that treads this day on ground" (63), one whose "huge anguish / [. . .] no tongue can well vnfold," and whose "haplesse fate" was never heard of before (73-74, 98).[158]

---

[158] I think Harris and Steffen's reference to the "likeness in their [Alcyon's and the narrator's] egocentric conceptions of their grief" (34) is the product of their failure to consider the narrator's statement in its entirety. Forgetting that he premises two crucial words, "Of *many*" (*Daphnaida* 37; emphasis mine), to his complaint, Harris and Steffen argue that the narrator "claims that he is the 'most miserable man' alive" (34).

The idea of the universality of the experience of loss attendant on the common human condition of fallenness receives great emphasis in Spenser's work. His texts often contrast his suffering characters' inclination to see their own situation as uniquely unhappy and themselves as the only targets for life's blows with reminders that single tragedies are proof of a general law of necessity running more or less as follows: given the premises that human beings are fallen and live in a fallen world, life in general can only be "wretched" (*Daphnaida* 9). In Spenser's narratives individual experiences of suffering, disillusionment and despair are usually set in the wider context of a universal and eternal chain of misery, a necessary chain for it inheres in the human condition. Life is often represented as marked by suffering from beginning to end as in *Ruines of Time* 47-49 where Spenser appropriates the biblical image of humans in tears from birth to death:

> [. . .] like as at the ingate of their berth,
> They crying creep out of their mothers woomb,
> So wailing backe go to their wofull toomb.[159]

Similarly, *Teares of the Muses* 159-62 dramatizes the existential course common to all human beings: all enter "the world with weeping eye" and after they have spent a certain number of days which "like dolorous Trophees, / Are heapt with spoyles of fortune and of feare," they are finally "laid forth on balefull beare." So, in between the bitter weeping at birth and at death, between the "first comming to the world" and the exit on a "beare," between the "woomb" and the "toomb," people must expect to face painful trials.

---

[159] Having described how he entered the world in tears, the author of the Wisdom of Solomon then comments: "All men then haue one entrance unto life, and a like going out" (7.6). One often finds the same concept expressed by classical writers: Seneca, for instance, says that humans wail both at birth and in point of death (letter 102.26). Shakespeare's Lear appropriates the biblical image in his address to the grieving Gloucester: "Thou must be patient; we came crying hither: / Thou know'st the first time that we smell the air / We wawl and cry," (*King Lear* 4.6.174-76).

A crucial passage in Book 2 of *The Faerie Queene* develops the theme that this is the common lot of the whole of humanity and not just of some particularly unlucky persons. When, having buried the suicide Amavia together with her husband, Guyon takes their little child into his arms, the Babe's smile, betraying his ignorance of his parents' "sad Tragedie" (2.2.1) and his own unhappy situation, moves the knight to tears and suggests to him a bitter reflection which at first centres upon the present particular case, but soon extends to the human condition in general. Addressing the "lucklesse babe," Guyon first laments his fate by describing him as one "borne vnder cruell starre, / And in dead parents balefull ashes bred," then tells him (but in reality his words are a meditation out aloud, as the child is too young to understand) "Full litle weenest thou, what sorrowes are / Left thee for portion of thy liuelihed" (2.2.2).

Up to this point, Guyon's words could well seem just a logical and realistic prophecy, given the child's situation as the orphaned son of a suicide and a man who died in dramatic circumstances, but it is not so and I believe Spenser masterly moves from particular to universal by means of a beautiful simile inspired by an immensely popular biblical image depicting the lot of humanity in general: the child is like a "budding braunch rent from the natiue tree, / And throwen forth, till it be withered" (2.2.2).[160] At last, voicing clearly what so far he had im-

---

[160] The image from Job 14 was very popular. Becon opens his widely read *ars moriendi* with a reference to it: "O full truly is it said of the holy man Job, [. . .]: 'Man that is born of a woman hath but a short time to live, [. . .]. He cometh up and withered away again like a flower" (*Sicke Mannes Salue* 92). Weatherby points out that "Spenser's 'natiue tree' in its most obvious signification is the 'senselesse truncke' of Mordant and Amavia, but it may also refer to the Tree of Life in the midst of Paradise, from which Adam's sin cut off his progeny" (338). Cf. the parable of the pruned vine in John 15.4-6 that Hamilton, in his 2001 edition of the *Faerie Queene*, indicates as the source for the Spenserian image, "If a man abide not in me, he is cast forth as a branche and withereth" (171). In the light of the context of the episode, I think Spenser's image suggests also the idea of change that brings decay, of mutability as mortality.

plied, Guyon declares he believes "such is the state of men: thus enter wee / Into this life with woe, and end with miseree" (2.2.2).[161] The trenchant statement, "such is the state of men," closing the stanza as an epitome, suggests the previous lines too are to be read as referring simultaneously to the Babe as a particular individual and to humanity in general. Ruddymane is said to have been "in dead parents balefull ashes bred" (2.2.2), but so are all human beings, since, as I believe, "dead" here means both 'physically dead' like the child's parents and the potential for spiritual death which threatens all humans after the Fall, and the term "parents" is assigned a triple semantic value as it alludes in the first place to Amavia and Mordant, but also to Adam and Eve, the common parents of all, and to all historical biological parents as transmitters of the original sin.[162] In the light of this stanza's universality, the "sorrowes" Guyon thinks will certainly embitter Ruddymane's life are merely his share of the existential store common to all humans. To ignore, as Alcyon does, one's share in the misery inherent in human fallenness, is also to ignore one's inclusion in the divine scheme of redemption.

Daphnaida develops the view that worldly perspectives produce false apprehensions of and inappropriate responses to suffering. Failing to see trials as necessary stages along the earthly path leading people back to God, as the narrative of Contemplation in Book 1 of *The Faerie Queene* represents them, Alcyon displays impatience. He goes so far as to question God's equity towards his creatures and his concern for them:

---

[161] Cf. *Teares of the Muses* 159-62 and *Ruines of Time* 47-49 quoted above. The recurrence of this image in different works signals its importance for Spenser.

[162] This reading is, I believe, legitimized by the symbolic function of the unwashable stains on Ruddymane's hands. Hamilton (among others) sees them as a sign of the permanence, proclaimed by Protestants, of the original sin even after baptism (1977 edition of the *FQ* 182-83). Alastair Fowler reads the entire episode as an allegory of baptism: "What is the burial of Mordant-Amavia but a burial of the 'old man'?" (143).

> What man henceforth that breatheth vitall aire,
> Will honour heauen, or heauenly powers adore?
> Which so vniustly do their iudgements share;
> Mongst earthly wights, as to afflict so sore
> The innocent, as those which do transgresse,
> And doe not spare the best or fairest, more
> Than worst or fowlest, but doe both oppresse.
>
> (Daphnaida 197-203)

Alcyon's complaint echoes Amavia's in Book 2 of *The Faerie Queene* where she accuses "heauens" of carelessness for innocent sufferers whose cause they do not champion, evident in the fact that they "despise / The doome of iust reuenge" (2.1.36). Amavia's accusations are reminiscent of the charges Job makes against God when he denounces His indifference and unwillingness to champion justice, "Beholde, I crie out of violence, but I haue none answere: I crie, but there is no iudgement" (Job 19.7). But whereas Job functions as a model for Christians facing painful trials because his impatience is followed by a demonstration of trust in God's providence and mercy, Amavia's suicide dramatizes the consequences of merely fleshly perspectives.

Following orthodox religious teaching, Spenser's contemporary readers would view Amavia and Alcyon's references to God's indifference (Amavia and Alcyon employ exactly the same terms, "carelesse heauens," *FQ* 2.1.36; *Daphnaida* 354) as blasphemous and their protests against God as a sign of their failure to perceive the gulf between "human and divine understanding of justice" and recognize that "only God has true perspective on his acts" (Harris and Steffen 32).[163]

---

[163] The narrative of the giant leveller (*FQ* 5.2) develops the view of the human incapacity to understand divine justice (see the excellent discussion by Mark Hazard). Calvin says that when they suffer famine, disease or bereavement "men curse their life, loathe the day of their birth, abominate heaven and the light of day, rail against God, and as they are eloquent in blasphemy, accuse him of injustice and cruelty" (1: 701). Regarding Amavia's and Alcyon's view of God's lack of concern for his creatures, it is worth noting that theo-

III Bereavement and Elegy 125

The falseness of the view that the state of human affairs signals God's lack of concern for and equity towards his creatures is highlighted in Boethius's *De consolatione philosophiae*. In Book 4 Philosophy asserts that all events fit into God's providential plan. She allows that Providence is "largely hidden from men, whose mind cannot understand the workings of the divine mind," but she urges Boethius to believe that "because it is conceived by God, it must be ultimately and perfectly just." Hence "Fate, the unfolding of Providence in the temporal world, may appear unjust, but this injustice is only apparent, not real, in its cosmic perspective" (both qtd. in Cherniss 14).[164]

In his sinful presumption to know what justice really is, Alcyon feels he is suffering injustice and laments his "vndeserued paines," his "vndeseru'd distresse" (522, 531). He calls his pains "vndeserued" as if he were ignorant of the link between the Fall and the state of human affairs. Churchmen insisted on the concept that human tribulations are indeed deserved, first of all because, together with death, they are both a manifestation and a consequence of the curse put by God on mankind following Adam's fault and also because they are a punishment of individual sins.[165] In this perspective, Christians should never feel

---

logians warned that on the occasion of "adversities [. . .] the devil putteth such phantasies" in the head of people "as though God would not intend them, or had somewhat else to do" (Latimer 1: 144). Perkins points to the "vilenesse, and uglinesse" of blasphemy which, he says, earn it the name of "foule tentation [sic]" (*Whole Treatise* 39).

[164] Cherniss's study offers a convenient summary of Boethius's text together with interesting comments on crucial passages and references to its popularity in the Renaissance.

[165] Becon declares that tribulations are both a consequence of the original sin "through the which disobedience and transgression of God's commandment, death and curse came over all mankind" (*Solace* 579) and a punishment of personal sins: Epaphroditus comments upon his fatal disease thus "God punisheth me justly for my sins" (*Sicke Mannes Salue* 105). I have chosen to quote from Becon once more because I find his expositions always very clear, but in the writings of all the other religious authorities of the time

wronged and depict themselves as victims of a cruel divinity.[166] Furthermore, theologians underlined that suffering, far from pointing to God's indifference or pitilessness, is a sure sign of his love and concern for his creatures, for in sending tribulations, God gives people a chance to meditate upon their sins, repent and prepare to receive his saving grace. "For whom the Lorde loueth, he chasteneth: and he scourgeth euery sonne whom hee receiueth" (Hebrews 12.6). Hence, because afflictions are signs of God's "good-will, love, and favour toward us" and are meant for his creatures' "commodity and salvation," Christians should be grateful and accept them willingly, they should not "murmur and grudge against God" (Becon, *Sicke Mannes Salue* 95, 94, 90), but instead show a godly "submission and subjection to the good pleasure of God" (Perkins, *Salve* 513).

Daphnaida and other Spenserian narratives (especially the narratives of *The Faerie Queene* that dramatize momentary breakdowns of even the most courageous heroes) present as difficult to imitate the model of the good Christian depicted in devotional works, that is, one who displays perfect patience and accepts all that happens without complaining (a model Daphne bodies forth). However, the majority of Spenser's suffering characters are equally incapable of imitating the Stoic model proposed by contemporary ideology under the influence of classical philosophy. The true Stoic never protests or revolts against what befalls him, because he knows that "whatever happens is in conformity with God's will and fulfills the plan of divine Reason" and hence recognizes that "there is a moral order in the universe" (Monsarrat 10, 11).[167] Often lacking such certainty, Spenser's sufferers tend to

---

whose works I have read one finds nearly identical views of afflictions as a form of punishment and correction and not as fortuitous mishaps.

[166] Thus Myles Coverdale: "Impatient folks grudge against God, pouring out all unthankfulness [. . .] and so imagine they in themselves a terrible and cruel God; yea all manner of vices grow out of impatiency" (96).

[167] Cf. Seneca: "In contrariety lies the cosmic permanence. To this law we must adjust our spirit: this law it must follow, this law obey. Whatever happens it must take as bound to happen, and refrain from scolding nature. What can't

see irrationality, disorder, chance, and lack of purpose behind events. Undoubtedly, they do not perceive evils as ultimately beneficial and advantageous, according to the lesson taught by philosophers whose views, on this point, coincide with those of Christian theologians: Boethius asserts that "any fortune which seems difficult either tests virtue or corrects and punishes vice" (99), and the sixteenth-century neo-Stoic Lipsius declares that "these grieuous afflictions sent of God do commonly either exercise the good, chastice offenders or punish the wicked; and al this for our good" (148).[168] Spenser's work teaches the lesson of endurance, but at the same time it emphasizes how difficult the task is for frail mortals facing daily trials. Spenser's narratives develop the view that a constant effort to hold on to the perspectives of faith by viewing things through the eye of the spirit is the only bulwark against despair. No Spenserian text dramatizes more clearly than *Daphnaida* the tight link between fleshly views and utter despair.

Given his careful construction of *Daphnaida*'s meaning through studied departures from formal and thematic decorum, the unusual place Spenser assigns the description of Daphne's blessedness is significant. Whereas visions of the dead's beatitude are usually found at the close of pastoral elegies (as in "November"), when the initial stages of "praise, demonstration of loss, lament" have been covered and a poetic crescendo signals the attainment of "consolation," in *Daphnaida* depiction of Daphne's bliss is given a central position

---

be cured is best endured: and best also it is to cleave uncomplainingly to God, the creator from whom all things come: it's a poor soldier who groans as he follows his commander" (letter 107.9, 2: 220).

[168] No widely read devotional work in Spenser's time fails to stress the ungodliness of attributions of afflictions to "chance" or "misfortune." As Patch points out, churchmen strongly opposed "belief in the casual" because it "carried with it the assumption that just so much territory lay outside of the province of the Christian God" (15). Patch's is a fine study of the classical origin of the idea of fortune and its popularity in Medieval and Renaissance Europe.

(lines 379-81).[169] G. W. Pigman is partly right when he says that "by placing Daphne's vision at the very center of the poem Spenser is affirming its superiority" (78), but I think this is also Spenser's way of pointing to Alcyon's lack of spiritual perspectives.[170] In fact, Alcyon's mood before and after his own reference to Daphne's blessedness (ll. 379-81), and his recollection of her dying words in which she expressed hopeful and joyful expectation of eternal bliss (263-92), is utter despair.

Spenser emphasizes the contrast between Alcyon's multiple references to immortality and celestial bliss and his hopelessness. He calls Daphne his "Saint" and acknowledges she "ioyeth in eternall blis" (379, 381), but these and other orthodox statements sound as empty formulae in his mouth, as his attitude and behaviour clearly signal his failure to grasp the full scope and significance of what he says and act upon it. The fact that he is not consoled points to his inclination to adopt an earthly perspective and failure to hold on to a celestial one. Alcyon figures forth the "old man" who is immoderately attached to things of this world and cannot accept their loss, who cannot "lift vp [his] heauie clouded eyne" (*Hymn of Heavenly Love* 222). Deaf to Daphne's references to immortality, he concentrates on mortality. In fact, he tells the narrator that whenever he recalls Daphne's last address to him, the image that presents itself to his mind is that of her "pallid cheekes and ashie hew," "hollow eyes and deadly view" (302, 304). With Daphne's hopeful and joyful words about resurrection still in his ears, Alcyon dwells on the memory of her corpse. Failing to view Daphne's death within the divine scheme of things, he concen-

---

[169] For Scaliger's description of the pattern of traditional elegies, see footnote 130 above.

[170] Commenting on the centrality of the description of Daphne's bliss within his careful analysis of *Daphnaida*'s numerological structure, Kay points out that "The poem as a whole contains nine climaterics, 9x63 lines, which presumably is meant to argue for a fitness in the death of Alcyon's wife, that it is the expression of higher orders and laws, in ways that are at present inaccessible to the understanding of the afflicted husband" (50).

trates on the aspects of death he perceives through his "fleshly eye" (*Hymn of Heavenly Beautie* 23). Overlooking the ultimate consequence of Daphne's death, her bliss, Alcyon focuses on its contingent effects: his loss, loneliness, and sorrow.

I think the centrality of Daphne's portrayal within *Daphnaida*'s structure signals the importance of the comparison between her and Alcyon within the elegy's persuasive strategy. Daphne is the pattern of the regenerate person who, seeing things through the eye of the spirit, displays patience, acceptance of the human condition, and awareness of the significance of life and death within the divine scheme. Against this ideal, Alcyon's earthliness that produces false responses to life and death appears clearly. Like Becon's Epaphroditus in the *Sicke Mannes Salue* and the other champions of the good death in contemporary *artes moriendi*, Daphne displays a ready and complete acceptance of God's will: since he has sent his messenger to her, summoning her to the "bridale feast" (268), she will "straight obay his soueraine beheast" (270). She shows no sign of protest or revolt against such a premature call (Lady Douglas Howard died when she was not yet nineteen). After all, what she sees in front of her is a door opening onto the realm of eternal bliss to which she firmly believes she is about to be admitted, in fact she affirms she will soon be "amongst those blessed ones," the "Saints and Angels" (287, 285) who incessantly sing God's praise. In the light of the transcendent significance she attributes to death as provider of true life, Daphne scolds Alcyon, albeit tenderly as the possessive "my" indicates, and shows him how irrational and ungodly his desperate grief is: "Ah why does my *Alcyon* weepe and mourne, / [. . .] / As if to me had chaunst some euill tourne?" (264-66).[171]

---

[171] It should be noticed that the language and argument Spenser uses here as well as in "November" 173-74 (see my comment in Chapter 8 above), are strikingly similar to the language and argument Becon employs to show that in the perspective of faith, crying for the dead is irrational and ungodly. In the rhetorical question already quoted above but worth a repetition here for its striking similarity to Daphne's, Becon's dying Christian wonders why

Daphne accepts willingly her own death and her share in mortality, in the conviction that what she leaves does not bear comparison with what she gains (lines 272-87). Her attitude of godly detachment from things of this world is very different from Alcyon's loathing of them. While Daphne expects no fulfilment or lasting joy from this life, since she knows that "nought on earth may lessen or appease" people's "miserie" (276, 272), Alcyon curses all that is earthly because it fails to meet his need for permanence and fulfilment. His declaration of hatred for life "because it will not last" and death "because it life doth marre" (425, 426), signals the earthliness of his perspective, since in the light of faith earthly life's limited duration is what allows for enjoyment of eternal life after death, which therefore does not mar life, but endows it with sense and direction. Failing to recognize that stasis would keep all things forever in their fallen state, Alcyon concludes "So all the world, and all in it I hate, / Because it changeth euer too and fro" (428-29). His final curse is for mutability, which he sees merely as an agent of disorder and not as God's agent in bringing everything back to him as the final stanzas of the *Mutabilitie Cantos* suggest.

As I have already indicated, Alcyon is not the only Spenserian character whose apprehension of mortality and mutability's presence at the core of life grows more intense and painful on the occasion of bereavement, arousing despair and loathing of life. The crucial difference between him and the other Spenserian bereaved with the exception of Amavia, who commits suicide, and the Stella of *Astrophel*, who dies of a broken heart, however, is that whereas for them this is a stage in the process that leads to their acceptance of the inevitability of life and death, and to consolation, Alcyon is immured in such a condition. The difference emerges neatly when one sets Alcyon's attitude against that of Una when she thinks Redcrosse has died. Both express loathing of mortal and mutable life, both despair and manifest loss of

---

people should cry for him: "Why for me? Because good things haue chaunced vnto me?" (*Sicke Mannes Salue* 124).

III Bereavement and Elegy 131

will to live. But whereas Una, having given vent to her grief, overcomes despair in the name of reason and faith, Alcyon never does.

Everywhere else presented as a champion of courage and endurance, in Book 1, canto 7 Una is overwhelmed by grief when she thinks Redcrosse is dead. Employing exactly the same metonymy as the despairing Amavia, she describes life as a "loathed light" (1.7.22; 2.1.36). Having used the word "light" for "life," Una then appropriately expresses her desire of death as a desire not to see anymore, hence she urges her eyes, the "dreary instruments of dolefull sight" (1.7.22), to close forever. She declares she wants to be spared two sights mainly, one being the "deadly spectacle" of Redcrosse's armour brought back by the Dwarf, a visible sign of the tragedy she thinks has befallen him and consequently herself too, the other is the sight of the "earthly mould," of all that is mortal.[172] She makes clear she rejects life because it brings pain and is inhabited by mortality. She beseeches the "senselesse cold" of death to freeze her capacity to feel and hence to suffer, she longs for the darkness of that "eternall night" to cover "so sad sight," life's misery, to make it invisible (1.7.22). Since she believes "earthly sight can nought but sorrow breed," she declares she wants her eyes "seeled vp with death" (1.7.23): this is indeed a straightforward presentation of life as an evil and death as its remedy.

Grief has maddened Una and led her into a mood of impatience and despair which she partly overcomes by giving vent to her feelings. "At last when feruent sorrow slaked was, / She vp arose" (1.7.28): though still grieving, Una regains self-mastery. Like the other Spenserian narratives of bereavement in *The Faerie Queene* and in the November eclogue of the *Calender*, the episode of Una's mourning dramatizes the healing function of displays of grief. Virtuous mourners in Spenser's texts regain self-control and the will to live after they have given expression to their woe. But the context of the narratives makes it clear

---

[172] In his 1977 edition of the *FQ*, Hamilton gives "body" and "earth" as pertinent meanings of the term "mould" in the present context and translates "earthly mould" as "mortal things" (101).

that while displays of sorrow, however extreme, are both useful and understandable in the initial phase of mourning, they must not be indulged to excess.[173] Though allowing that Una has "great cause of plaint, / That stoutest heart [. . .] could cause to quake" (1.7.52), Arthur presses her with a series of warnings and words of encouragement (sts. 38, 40, 41, and 42) aimed at rousing her from the mood of self-pity and indulgence in despair signalled by her description of herself as "the laughing stocke of fortunes mockeries" (1.7.43) and her comment that there is nothing left for her to do than her "woes to weepe and waile" (st. 39).

At last Arthur points out to Una that despair is overcome through faith: "Despaire breedes not (quoth he) where faith is staid," and when she advances the argument of frailty, "No faith so fast [. . .] but flesh does paire," Arthur replies: "Flesh may empaire [. . .] but reason can repaire" (st. 41).[174] *Daphnaida* implicitly reiterates Arthur's lesson for its putative audience of obsessive grievers; whenever Alcyon's mortal perspectives and lack of self-mastery are emphasized, in fact, the perspectives of faith and rule of reason are implicitly evoked.

Nowhere in Spenser's work is holding on to these perspectives represented as an easy task. The Spenserian narratives put characters through a series of trials and tribulations that put their endurance to a

---

[173] Spenser's texts always represent bereavement as a very painful experience and dramatize the therapeutic function of violent manifestations of sorrow by mourners. The fiction of Calidore's supposed bereavement in *FQ* 6.11 is an illuminating example. When he is told that Pastorella is dead, his "wits with doole were nigh distraught": Calidore beats his head and breast, contemplates suicide and curses "th'heauens" (st. 33). He regains self-mastery and resumes action "after griefe awhile had had its course, / And spent it selfe in mourning" (st. 34). Provided it does not become chronic, the temporary maddening of bereaved characters is not censured in Spenser's work and is often represented sympathetically.

[174] "All the passions of the soul should be regulated according to the rule of reason, which is the root of virtuous good" (Aquinas, 2.q.39.art.2, 1: 791). Aquinas says that "excessive sorrow [. . .] consumes the soul; for such sorrow paralyzes the soul, and hinders it from shunning evil" (art. 3, 1: 791).

severe test. Despite their constant, hence exhausting, efforts at holding on to the perspectives of faith and to the rule of reason, even champions of courage and patience, like Una, at times collapse. In this light, Alcyon's perception of the misery of the human condition per se is dramatized as neither wrong, nor excessively pessimistic. As ever, it is the perspective taken that Spenser's reader is asked to judge. Whereas the likes of Daphne clearly see the painfulness of this life as a pointer to celestial bliss, Alcyon is incapable of seeing the Christian antithesis to "this worlds vainnesse and lifes wretchednesse" (34) and thus remains immured in his loathing of his present state.

The picture of life Daphne draws is appalling. The main part of her dying speech, in fact, is an exposition of the view that it is more natural and rational to long for death than to love life, since "our daies are full of dolour and disease, / Our life afflicted with incessant paine," "why then should I desire here to remaine?" (274-75, 277). Daphne defines her short life as a "long imprisonment" (273), thus expressing in other words the same idea one finds in Seneca: "what lies between our first day and our last is variable and uncertain: count the hardships, and it's long even for a boy" (letter 99.9, 2: 176). Daphne declares she sees death as a "wished rest" free from "worlds sad care [and] wasting woe" (282, 283). She says she finally sets off with "gladnesse" for this peaceful haven, having "long desired" to get there (282, 281).

In keeping with his inclination to perceive just half of the whole picture, Alcyon, the addressee of this confession, overlooks the explicit references to hope and belief in an afterlife of bliss that accompany Daphne's comment on life's wretchedness. Hence he feels Daphne's "last deadly accents" as "piercing words" which like "swords" have wounded his heart and rent his "bleeding chest" (297, 295, 297, 298). What he retains of his wife's last speech is her terrible judgement on life, a judgement he appropriates when he says "to liue I finde it deadly dolorous" (449). In this light, death appears utterly desirable and in fact Alcyon declares he longs for it, since he believes "sorrow should haue end thereby, / And cares finde quiet" (446-47). Daphne's godly desire of death and Alcyon's censurable death-wish arising from mere escapism, are juxtaposed. Whereas Daphne accepts patiently God's summons, Alcyon impatiently entreats death to come: "To carelesse heauens [he] daylie call[s]" for his "confusde decay" (354, 353). Whereas young Daphne is portrayed as she joyfully goes to meet death, which she desires both as release from life's miseries and as a passage to heaven, Alcyon is pictured as he reluctantly decides to resist his suicidal urges in order to keep the promise made to Daphne, "I must stay [. . .], / My *Daphne* hence departing bad me so," thus preparing to "liue in lifes despight" (442).[175]

Alcyon overlooks another important passage of Daphne's last message: she urges him to love their little child, Ambrosia, a "pledge" (288) of their love, a symbol of its survival and of the continuance of life after her death.[176] Daphne's exhortation to Alcyon to take care of the child expresses her hope that he will be reasonable in his grief and will reintegrate himself into the mainstream of life, resuming his duty. Although Ambrosia is never mentioned again, the reader is led to think that Alcyon's choice to "withdraw [. . .] to some darkesome place, / Or some deepe caue, or solitarie shade" (486-87) is hardly compatible with fulfilment of paternal duties.[177] Moreover, reference to Alcyon's abandonment of his flock to its fate (lines 344-50) signals

---

[175] Amavia refuses to "liue in liues despight" (*FQ* 2.1.36; note that Amavia and Alcyon employ exactly the same expression) and chooses to commit suicide in the conviction that "carelesse heauens" who "take delight / To see sad pageants of mens miseries" cannot "warne death from wretched wight" (2.1.36).

[176] As regards the name Ambrosia (the actual name of the Gorges's daughter), Donald Cheney points to its significance as "celestial food" and argues that "Spenser seems to have seized on it for the obvious irony in having ambrosia the gift offered the grieving husband rather than to the dead and transfigured wife" ("Spenser's Fortieth Birthday" 12).

[177] Amavia too forsakes her duties as mother. Both narratives, Amavia's and Alcyon's, dramatize the consequences of self-centred grief and self-absorption.

that besides his private duties, he also forsakes his social and public ones.[178]

Spenser's narratives (that of Timias is a perfect example) represent the inclination of grievers to opt out of life and shun society as understandable but inappropriate. Rejection of the world out of disillusion signals false perspectives as it is the product of one's failure to recognize the fallenness of the world and accept the fact that, being fallen, it cannot match human expectations. Unwilling to endure the necessary hurts of life, Spenser's impatient sufferers abandon the world that has disappointed them. The context of the narratives implies the readerly response that they should rather examine the appropriateness of their expectations than blame the world for not being what they would want it to be. The inclination to protest against mortality, instead of adjusting one's view of and responses to it, is censured throughout Spenser's work and especially, as I will demonstrate in the following chapter, in works belonging to the collection of *Complaints*.

---

[178] He wastes his poetic gifts as well. In *Colin Clovts Come Home Againe* Alcyon is described as still "bent to mourne, / Though fit to frame an euerlasting dittie" (384-85). This confirms that what is censured about Alcyon's grief is not its intensity but its chronic persistence.

IV
The Sight of Ruins and the "Sabaoths Sight"

10. Melancholy and Complaints

As I have demonstrated in the previous chapter, *Daphnaida* is neither an unsuccessful, nor a successful elegy: it is something else. It is a dramatization of the dismay, impatience and despair that arise from a fleshly view of life and death. From a formal point of view, it is a long complaint about ruined hopes and unfulfilled expectations. Variable in length, written as independent compositions or inserted in larger narrative frames, complaints about the "ruins of life" recur in the whole Spenserian canon. What they all have in common is the crucial fact that their speakers blame their dissatisfaction and suffering on the world which they see as the realm of vanity and corruption and never question the appropriateness of their attachments and expectations. The context of the narratives provides a different perspective suggesting that whereas they hold mutability responsible for their despair, it is really their views of it which condemn them to immurement in inconsolable melancholy.

It is my aim in the present chapter to argue that the literary form of complaint, extensively used in Spenser's work, suits the pervasive emphasis on human dissatisfaction that I have traced in *The Faerie Queene* and in *Daphnaida*. The mode is inflected to present inconsolable woefulness at the sight of ruins as sinful and largely self-inflicted, generated by lack of spiritual perspectives and attachment to ephemerae. What makes Spenser's treatment distinctive is that it focuses more on the psychological than on the spiritual consequences of this attitude. Spenser's texts dramatize as a hell on earth the experience of those who, immersed in life's troubled water, often fail to keep the "Sabaoths sight" in view. The plight of such characters is dramatized sympathetically in Spenser's narratives, but indulgence in melancholy and the expectation of fulfilment from things that "shall turne to dust" (*Hymne of Beavtie* 98) are nevertheless not condoned.

Since humans are "subject to infirmities, miseries [. . .], tossed and tumbled up and downe, carried about with every small blast," Robert Burton declares that "melancholy [. . .] is the Character of Mortalitie" (1: 136). To a certain extent, this is the view that Spenser's work dramatizes. The careful reader, however, detects ironies and implied censure in the Spenserian treatment of melancholic responses to the impermanence of earthly goods.

As I have shown in previous chapters, consideration of Spenser's whole work shows the extensive exploitation of one of the most popular ideological and literary topoi of the day, that of melancholy.[179] The recurrence of narratives of melancholy, the prominence given to melancholy characters who are often assigned a leading role and whose laments often take up most of the space (cf. Colin's complaints in the January and December eclogues of the *Calender*, Alcyon's in *Daphnaida*, the Muses' in *Teares of the Muses*, Clarion's in *Muiopotmos*, Verlame's in *Ruines of Time*) reflect the contemporary view of the frequency of melancholy and the general interest in it. As we have seen, his major work, *The Faerie Queene*, is often pervaded by melancholy; a large number of main and secondary characters beside Spenser's narrator utter melancholy reflections. It is my view, however, that this emphasis on the discourse of melancholy is a strategy to juxtapose fleshly and spiritual perspectives and elaborate their consequences.

The use in Spenser's work of the specific contemporary discourses of melancholy is highly selective. Spenser's references to medical views of the consequences of an excess of melancholy humour in the blood, for example, are neither more numerous, nor more accurate than those present in most sixteenth-century literary, moral and theological writings.[180] No trace, to my knowledge, is found of the phi-

---

[179] For an interesting analysis of the cultural significance of melancholy in early modern England, see Douglas Trevor's *The Poetics of Melancholy*.

[180] In fact, references to medical views of melancholy in Spenser's work are far less numerous or detailed than those found for instance in Shakespeare's

losophical apprehension of melancholy as a sign of genius.[181] The theological and often also medical emphasis on the supernatural causes of "the malady," when God or the devil or some spirits agitate the humours to various ends, has equally not left significant marks on Spenser's texts, except for the narrative of Redcrosse's suicidal despair in Book 1 of the *Faerie Queene*. What they inflict instead is the self-absorption, dissatisfaction, inclination to recrimination and weariness with duty that men of letters and authors of psychological tracts presented as characteristic of melancholy people.[182] While allowing for significant distinctions produced by the various contexts and programmes of Spenser's works, his melancholy characters or personae are characterized by their fixation with the past; both a remote, collective past which they see as the *locus* of virtue, innocence, and happiness, and a recent personal past rich in things irretrievably lost to which they had tied their expectations and on which they obsessively meditate. Their attitude to the present is one of loathing, since they see it as the climax of a progressive cosmic degeneration and as the occasion for new woes. Characteristically, they think that resistance to the flux of change through withdrawal from active life will spare them new losses.

The pervasiveness of the theme of melancholy is closely related to Spenser's extensive and often distinctive use, over twenty years of writing, of the literary form that best suits melancholy utterances: the

---

plays and even in religious writings such as Perkins's *Treatise of the Cases of Conscience*. For a discussion of Shakespearian references to humoral physiology, see Ruth L. Anderson's not recent, but amply documented *Elizabethan Psychology and Shakespeare's Plays* and David Hoeniger's *Medicine and Shakespeare in the English Renaissance*.

[181] "The Dignity of Melancholy" in Babb, *The Elizabethan Malady*, deals with the genesis and Renaissance views of "Aristotelian" melancholy.

[182] For standard medical and literary portraits of the malcontent, see Part Three, footnote 149.

complaint.[183] Defined by George Puttenham in his *Arte of English Poesie* (1589) as a poetic expression of feelings "contrary to rejoising," the complaint requires a melancholy speaker who regrets and laments the loss of "parents, frends, allies, and children, [. . .] of goods and worldly promotions, honour and good renowne," who recriminates over "the travails and torments of love forlorne or ill bestowed" and expresses dismay at "the subversions of townes and cities," briefly, one who weeps over the ruins of mortal and mutable life (qtd. in Vecchi 131).

To the genre of complaint, which takes its name from the Latin *planctus* (grieving or lamentation), belong medieval and Renaissance works of various lengths and metres, but sharing the same plaintive, and often moral and nostalgic, tone.[184] Spenser's many complaint poems belong to a range of traditions. Three of the nine poems in the *Complaints* collection belong to the *de casibus* tradition, deriving from Boccaccio's *De casibus virorum illustrium* and made immensely popular in England by Lydgate's *Falls of Princes* (1431), and the two versions of *A Myrroure for Magistrates* of 1559 and 1563: *The Ruines of Time* which dramatizes the illustrious lives and tragic deaths of members of the Dudley-Sidney family, *Virgils Gnat*, a version of the pseudo-Virgilian *Culex*, where the fate of Greek and Trojan heroes illustrates the "chaungfull turning of mens slipperie state" (554), and *Muiopotmos*, where the narrator meditates on the vanity of Clarion's pride in his beauty and pre-eminence.

---

[183] The *Complaints* collection includes pieces written between 1569 and 1590, see Richard McCabe's edition of Spenser's shorter poems 580-82.

[184] The scriptural and classical sources, conventions and function of the complaint literature are discussed in Kerrigan 1-86. I am indebted to this discussion for my own survey in the following paragraphs. Kerrigan reproduces a number of complaints dating from the Middle Ages to the eighteenth century. Peter's *Complaint and Satire in Early English Literature* deals with the influence of Latin, French and Italian works on English complaints. Chapter 4 is a helpful analysis of the moral themes of complaint.

IV The Sight of Ruins and the "Sabaoths Sight"

Five of the *Complaints*, on the other hand, derive more directly from a tradition that emphasizes the fallenness of humanity and the world, their subjection to corruption and decay. This is the *contemptus mundi* tradition whose most influential example is the *De miseria humanae conditionis* (1195) by Cardinal Lotario dei Segni (later pope Innocent III). Complaints by Spenser that can be placed in this tradition are: *Teares of the Muses*, which laments the postlapsarian state of the world where virtue and the arts are scorned, *Ruines of Rome*, a translation from Du Bellay, where the fate of the greatest empire ever exemplifies the necessary end of all that is subject to time and mutability, *Visions of the Worlds Vanitie*, a self-explicatory title, and the sonnets Spenser translates from Du Bellay and Petrarch, which develop the view that everything earthly is "nought but flying vanitee" and "onely God surmounts all times decay" (*Visions of Bellay* 11, 13) and urge readers to "loath this base world, and thinke of heauens blis" (*Visions of Petrarch* 96).

Finally a tradition that in Spenser's England was developing into social satire with works such as George Gascoigne's *Steele Glas* (1576) and Thomas Lodge's *Fig for Momus* (1595) was that of complaints about the evils of the time and the corruption in the church and at court. This tradition contributes to the May, July and September eclogues of the *Calender* which deal with clerical abuses, and to *Prosopopoia, or Mother Hubberds Tale* which deals with ecclesiastical, courtly, and monarchical shortcomings. The proems to Books 5 and 6 of *The Faerie Queene* are often cited examples of complaints against the degeneration of present times.[185]

My contention is that Spenser makes a distinctive use of the complaint mode to develop the view that false expectations more than the sway of mutability and mortality are responsible for human despair before loss. His strategy is most clearly visible in the *Shepheardes Calender* and in *Ruines of Time*.

---

[185] Mine is a general classification of Spenser's complaints; such works as *Teares of the Muses* fall into more than one category.

11. Colin's "Worldly Sorow" (2 Cor. 7.10)

The *Shepheardes Calender* opens with a long plaintive soliloquy by a "pale and wanne" ("January" 8) love-melancholic who "compareth his carefull case to the sadde season of the yeare" (Argument) and weeps on his ruined youth, "but now my spring begonne, / And yet alas, yt is already donne" (29-30). References to his "life bloud friesing with vnkindly cold," his "balefull smart," and his "lustfull leafe [which] is drye and sere" (26, 27, 37) arouse sympathy for the grieving shepherd. The second half of his complaint, however, suggests that Colin's self-centredness and indulgence in grief are partly responsible for his despair: his "timely buds with *wayling* are all *wasted*," his "blossome [. . .] / With breathed *sighes* is *blowne away*" (38-40; emphases mine), his "mind is ouercome with care," he says "with mourning pyne I" (46, 48). He is so absorbed in grief that he neglects his duty; his "ill gouernement" of his flock is the cause of its poor state (45). He also wastes his poetic gifts and immures himself in grief, "so broke his oaten pype, and downe dyd lye" (72). When in the August eclogue Cuddie sings a song "that Colin made" (142), the self-willed character of Colin's woe and his morbid desire to grieve are emphasized. In Cuddie's voice Colin says "let stremes of teares supply the place of sleepe: / [. . .] and all that may augment / My doole, drawe neare" (163-65). He declares he will spend the rest of his life alone the better to concentrate on his woe, "more meete to wayle my woe, / Bene the wild woddes my sorrowes to resound" (165-66). He plans "all the night in plaints, the daye in woe / [. . .] to wayst" (179-80). 'Waste' is a significant verb in connection with Colin's design to opt out of life and live a living death.

Waste and loss are the themes of the December eclogue which "(euen as the first beganne) is ended with a complaynte of Colin" (Argument), a detail which confirms that fixity and lack of evolution are Colin's marks. The unwary reader may be easily moved by Colin's retrospective glance at life from the perspective of approaching death. He declares the passing of time has brought him no gift of wisdom –

IV The Sight of Ruins and the "Sabaoths Sight"   143

in fact he describes himself as "vnwise and witlesse" (91) – but rather bitter disillusionment, since he feels his youthful expectations of happiness have not been met: "and all my hoped gaine is turnd to scathe," "my haruest wast, my hope away dyd wipe" (100, 108).[186] Feeling death is not far off, Colin weighs the achievements of his life in the balance and finds that suffering and disappointments have exceeded by far the few moments of joy and sense of self-fulfilment, "of all my haruest hope I haue / Nought reaped but a weedy crop of care" (121-22).

It is possible, however, to detect the ironies and criticism implied in Colin's self-portrait. Since in "December" he is as young as in "January," still a "shepheards boye" ("January" 1), his world weariness seems excessive for his youth drawing attention to its rhetorical nature. For "December" Colin adopts an existing complaint, the *Eclogue au Roy* addressed to Francis I by an aged Marot. Harry Berger argues that "Spenser transforms Marot's motif of the older shepherd's retrospect into a trope, a hyperbole expressing the pathological pleasure in the rhetoric of self-pity that marks the victim's discourse."[187] Perhaps then Colin's complaint in the December eclogue about the vanity of life is not all that it seems.

Colin's contemplation of the ruins of his life is moving, "Of all the seede, that in my youth was sowne, / Was nought but brakes and brambles to be mowne" ("December" 101-02). This everyman who has gone through the cycle of the year with its succession of seasons that represents the span of mortal life, finds nothing has fulfilled his desires and hopes. Instead of looking beyond earthly life, he bemoans its limits. Like Alcyon in *Daphnaida* who is incapable of reorienting

---

[186] As regards Colin's self-portrait as "vnwise and witlesse" ("December" 91), McLane points out that "according to the principle of dramatic decorum, shepherds are rude and ignorant; hence not only their language, but also their knowledge and manners are faulty" (305). For the significance of Colin's "December" mood, see Louis Montrose 54-59.

[187] Berger 387. See Berger's suggestive discussion of Colin's fictitious ageing in *Revisionary Play* 416-41.

his expectations towards the spiritual direction shown in his wife's dying speech, Colin is equally in despair before his "weedye crop of care" (122), thus ignoring the significance of earthly harvest from the Christian perspective he himself evokes elsewhere in "December" through his reference to "Christmas" (26), and in "November," where he depicts the "fayre fieldes" where the blessed will "ioyes enioye [. . .], that mortall men doe misse" (188, 196). Compared to the Christian attitude of anticipation of eternal gain, his regret and recrimination signal his fleshliness.

According to the *Oxford English Dictionary*, Chaucer was the first to use "complaint" to mean an "outcry against or because of injury; [a] representation of wrong suffered; [an] utterance of grievance" (3). In this sense, Colin's utterance is a "rhetorical self-revelation" (Rasmussen 159).[188] Colin blames the "shepheards God" who did "ill vpbraide [his] hurtlesse pleasaunce" ("December" 50-51). He depicts himself as an innocent victim.[189] In "June" he had already and more openly blamed his unhappiness on "cruell fate, / And angry Gods" who, he says, "pursue [him] from coste to coste" (14-15). That is why, he thinks, he is excluded from "that Paradise [. . .], whych *Adam* lost" where Hobbinoll lives happily "withouten dreade of Wolues" ("June" 10, 12). To mistake the earth for Eden, hence denying the world's fallenness, is an attitude that signals lack of spiritual perspectives. No happy place free from danger, corruption, and decay, exists on earth since God's "haplesse curse" has turned it into a wilderness where "Wolues and Thieues abound" (*FQ* 7.6.55). Not fate, fortune or angry gods are the cause of Colin's despair, but his own false expectations. It is the folly of expecting that his "spring would euer laste" that makes Colin more painfully aware of "wintrye ages waste" ("Decem-

---

[188] Rasmussen uses the expression quoted with reference to Verlame, the plaintive character in *Ruines of Time*.

[189] As we have seen, the Spenserian characters who hold fleshly views like Alcyon in *Daphnaida* and Amavia in *FQ* 2.1 tend to think of themselves as innocent victims of fate or God.

IV The Sight of Ruins and the "Sabaoths Sight" 145

ber" 30, 29), life's blows. He is as responsible of his woe as another Spenserian character, "careles *Clarion*," who equally expects to enjoy an eternal spring in a place free from danger (*Muiopotmos* 417, 418). The juxtaposition of descriptions of Clarion's attitude (he flies "careleslie" from flower to flower "fearles of foes and hidden ieopardie") and the place he takes for "Paradise" where evil in the shape of Aragnoll lays "lurking couertly him to surprise," signals his foolishness (391, 251, 186, 247). Only a "foolish Flie without foresight" ignores that nothing "can long abide in state" on the earth where "thousand perills lie in close awaite" (389, 221, 217).

From the plaintive eclogues of the *Calender* at the start of his poetic career, to *Muiopotmos* in the 1591 *Complaints* collection and the fiction of Calidore's pastoral retreat in Book 6 of the 1596 edition of *The Faerie Queene*, Spenser's poetry repeatedly develops the view that the Arcadian state of mind generates false expectations. A life untouched by change, death, loss, the consequences of the Fall, is not a possibility for fallen humans in the fallen world. Innocence and happiness in a Christian perspective are regained through spiritual regeneration, not through retreat. In this sense the Spenserian texts mentioned at the start of this paragraph express criticism of "pastoral states of mind," of the impulse to resist the flux of change by retreating to an imaginary world of static perfection (Berger 321).

As many scholars have observed, the *Calender* simultaneously exploits the literary fiction of the pastoral world and criticizes its ideological basis as false and unchristian, a threat to both spiritual and psychological wholesomeness.[190] Colin's "paradise principle" (Berger 278) is the source of his despair, because it leads him to invest everything in the here and now only to find that the expected harvest is

---

[190] A thoughtful treatment of Spenser's criticism of the ideology at the base of pastoral poetry is Berger's "Re-verting to the Green Cabinet," in *Revisionary Play*. Berger views the *Calender* as a "metapastoral," that is a work that "produces its effect by critically miming features of the genre it claims simultaneously to revive and to revise or overgo" (320).

wasted. Hence his inconsolable melancholy at the close of the December eclogue when he bids adieu to all he has lived for signals that he cannot, in Calvin's words, "cease to be stunned with a base and foolish admiration of it [the world], as if it contained in itself the ultimate goal of good things" (1: 714). His adieu does not express a holy *contemptus mundi*, but rather the Pauline "worldly sorow [which] causeth death" (2 Cor. 7.10). "Winter is come, [. . .], / And after Winter commeth timely death" ("December" 149-50); the sterility of Colin's closeness to the world that has failed to live up to his expectations immures him in a stasis that prevents his regeneration from the living death of fleshliness.

12. Fleshly and Spiritual Views of the *Ruines of Time*

The title of the emblem book Spenser had a hand in as a young translator appears to me perfectly to describe the view developed in Spenser's "complaint" writing. Jan van der Noodt's *Theatre* (1569) proposes to represent "the miseries and calamities that follow the voluptuous Worldlings, As also the greate ioyes and plesures which the faithfull do enioy." The tension between the views of the "wordlings" and those of the "faithfull" is a major source of inspiration for Spenser's poetry. By and large, the many complaints one finds throughout Spenser's work are all expressions of the point of view of the "wordlings" and hence, I suggest, are supposed to draw readers' attention to what the "faithfull" see. While the "wordlings" gaze disconsolately at ruins of all kinds, material and moral, the "faithfull" turn their eyes from ruins to the "pillours of Eternity" (*FQ* 7.8.2) that lie beyond them. Nowhere more explicitly than in *Ruines of Time*, the piece that opens Spenser's 1591 *Complaint* collection, are the two perspectives and their consequences juxtaposed.

Ruines of Time is an instructive poem about false and holy expressions of *contemptus mundi*, the first, spoken by Verlame, leading to immurement in melancholy and regret, the other, spoken by a voice addressing the narrator, leading to the awareness that humans are, in Erasmus's words, "wayfarynge men in this worlde, not inhabytantes" (*Preparation* A4^v). Both Verlame and the voice use the *vanitas* trope and evoke the effects of mutability's sway. Their descriptions of the status quo are similar, but their perspectives are divergent. And it is precisely on this hiatus that the poem's stress falls.

At first, the lament of Verlame, the sorrowful Genius of the ruined Roman city of Verulam, seems an orthodox repetition of the bitter descriptions of earthly affairs in Ecclesiastes. Like the author of Ecclesiastes whose complaint opens on consideration of the ruin of all the "woorkes that [his] hands had wrought" (2.11), then develops a view of universal vanity, "all is vanitie, and vexation of the spirite" (2.17), Verlame first laments her personal ruin, then states that hers is the fate of all that is earthly which "doth as a vapour vanish, and decaie" (*Ruines of Time* 36-42, 56).[191]

Verlame weeps over the fact that no physical or moral monument that humans erect is permanent. Great buildings people raise as visible, lasting signs of their power and prosperity sooner or later turn into "ruines" and "ashes" (39, 40) like the "houses" and "vineyards" that made the author of Ecclesiastes pre-eminent among his countrymen (Ecclesiastes 2.4). In this light, ruins function for future generations as visual lessons about transience and impermanence, "All such vaine moniments of earthlie masse, / Deuour'd of Time, in time to nought doo passe" (*Ruines of Time* 419-20). Powerful men and great thinkers of the past who seemed able in their own way to steer the course of history, are dead and often forgotten as all the answers Verlame gives to her own *ubi sunt* questions at lines 57-77 prove. "For there shall be no remembrance of the wise, not of the foole" (Ecclesiastes 2.16). This illustrates the point that "honour," "aduauncement," "worlds glorie," "wisedome" are "vaine" (*Ruines of Time* 51, 43, 60, 43), for when one dies everything he or she has striven after dies with him or her, "For deeds doo die, how euer noblie donne" (400). Even great empires, which are signs of human attempts to model space and events and direct human history along a chosen path, cannot withstand the overwhelming power of time and change, as the fall of the greatest of them all in Western eyes, the Roman, testifies. As Verlame observes, everything on earth is "but fained," nothing but a "vaine illusion" (204, 456): this view of the deceptive, illusory nature of all that is human and earthly, apart from its scriptural source in Ecclesiastes, is reminiscent of the Platonic description of the world as the realm of mere images and appearances, of unreality and instability. Human longing for the realm of Forms, for the stable, the permanent, the unchanging, the immortal, is constantly disappointed.

---

[191] Cf. James 4.14: "For what is your life? It is euen as a vapour that appeareth for a litle time, and afterward vanisheth away."

Whereas the author of Ecclesiastes overcomes sadness by accepting worldly things for what they are, enjoying them as provisional gifts of God whose ways are inscrutable (11.4-12), Verlame is dismayed and in tears before the collapse of all that humans build or value and attempts to find the reason behind what appears as time and mutability's meaningless destructive fury. She gets near to the truth later revealed in the vision when she declares people's crucial mistake is to think that what is mortal, whether fame or the products of human hands and mind, can bestow immortality, "how can mortall immortalitie giue?" (413). But, unable to draw her due conclusions from this right premise and from her own acknowledgement of a Christian perspective when she says of Leicester that "all is with him dead, / Saue what in heauens storehouse he vplaid" (211-12), Verlame is denied the vision of true transcendence in a religious dimension that is granted the narrator and places her trust instead in another form of human, hence mortal endeavour, poetry, whose power to bestow immortality the context of the narrative, as we shall see, disclaims. Verlame's rhetorical question uncovers the root of human frustrations and painful disillusions: it is the crucial mistake made by all Spenserian sufferers who expect that beings and things of this world can either become immortal or give access to immortality. Their experience figured in Spenser's verse teaches them that the more tenaciously they cling to ephemerae, the more intensely they suffer for their loss.[192]

The Christian context, made explicit or subtly implied, of Spenser's fictions highlights the short-sightedness of these observers of the state of things and stresses the limits of their views when all they see is the "Catastrophees" (*Teares of the Muses* 158) that daily hit humans, sweeping away all kinds of monuments they erect. The Christian framework of their narratives implies that the agents of destruction are

---

[192] "That that is spoken of ryches, the same is to be understood of honours, pleasures, wyfe, children, kynfolke, frendes, of beautie, youth, good helth. [. . .] The more fervently we loue a thynge, the more paynfully we be plucked frome it" (Erasmus, *Preparation* sig. A4).

the products of sin. But sin has not just brought devastation to the world, it has also occasioned Christ's coming: in this light, contemplation of ruins should generate awareness of the progress towards redemption and salvation. Verlame's pre-Christian perspective is of course different and brings no consolation. This progress is reflected very well in the poetic movement from the "tragicke Pageants" (490) illustrating the misery of life on earth (491-574), to the "other sights" (588) of resurrection and human release from transience and decay that are presented as visions to the narrator of *Ruines of Time* (589-672). What is implied by the second vision is that there is reason and meaning in all that happens; Providence is at work behind the seemingly fortuitous succession of events, and both world and humanity, though unaware, proceed along a linear path leading to redemption and death's death. This narrative is made explicit in the *Mutabilitie Cantos*.

By using the motif of a vision (the "other sights") revelatory of a divine perspective to correct the limited perception of reality expressed by Verlame that the vision of the "tragicke Pageants" (490) seems to confirm, *The Ruines of Time*, in common with other Spenserian works, fully exploits some implications of the term 'vision.'[193] A vision may imply something that goes beyond and lies outside the real, the physical; in this case, it is sent either by God, or it is obtained through magic or mystical practices. In the temple of Isis episode (*FQ* 5.7) Spenser exploits the meaning of vision as "a revelation, supernaturally presented to the mind either in sleep or in an abnormal state" (*OED* 1.a.) to create a fiction of Britomart's future. By allowing her an insight into the goals of her quest and destiny, the "wondrous vision" (5.7.12) stimulates Britomart's energetic pursuit of her task.

Visions may disclose what appear to be truths that are normally unknown to human beings and belong to an order of reality that is not

---

[193] On Spenser's use of the conventions of "vision poems," see the articles "Vision," "Visions," and "Dreams" by Hyde, Wittreich, and Schreirer in *Spenser Encyclopedia*.

human. Hence, by figuring the orthodox Christian explanation of the apparent meaningless and purposeless state of things in the shape of a vision (the "other sights" of lines 588-670), *Ruines of Time* dramatizes the idea that people cannot really fully understand or grasp this truth through the media they depend on for the exploration of their own world, that is sense, intellect, sensibility. Christianity, in fact, is a revealed religion. Those who, like Verlame, are granted no vision through faith are left confused and disconsolate, complaining against a state of things whose purpose and meaning they are unable to comprehend, while they are only too familiar with the suffering it causes to them and others.

Even those who have been shown in a vision that there is purpose and direction in earthly affairs and final redemption of the general corruption, the vision once vanished, have to reopen their eyes on the imperfect world around them. This, of course, the vision has left unchanged and even if a moment of enlightenment can make one see things differently, this perspective is difficult to retain when one is immersed in life. While the vision lasts everything seems clear, but visions are transitory as Calidore's brief contemplation of the Graces shows (*FQ* 6.10), and hope and faith may easily waver. What Spenserian characters are at times granted is just a vision, not the immediate transformation of what saddens them, nothing but the promise of a future transformation. This is often less than people need to face the workings of mortality day after day dry-eyed.

Furthermore, a vision can even make things worse, make it more difficult for people to accept the status quo. One may be left like Redcrosse who, having contemplated the heavenly Jerusalem, would rather not go back to Cleopolis, or Calidore who "had no will away to fare" (6.10.30). Consideration of the perfection, permanence, fulfilment that lies beyond can make Spenser's characters even more painfully aware of the corruption, impermanence, futility of everything that is mortal. "So darke are earthly things compard to things diuine" (1.11.67): this is the narrator's comment closing the canto where Redcrosse is shown the end of his "painefull pilgrimage" (1.10.61). The line sums up the view of life reiterated in Spenser's work. It would be a fit preamble to the narrator's final prayer in the *Cantos* to be granted a permanent vision of what lies beyond the "pillours of Eternity" (7.8.2), the perfect, the unfading, the immortal, the true.

Some visions, then, make people see that beyond the reality they know and live in lies another dimension where human limitations are finally annulled and expectations fulfilled. Spenser's texts develop the view, however, that such a perspective may comfort, but it may also deepen melancholy and awareness of the futility of all human endeavours. If perfection and permanence exist only beyond this life, all the myths of permanence civilizations in all ages have attempted to create in the shape of heaped stones or great works of art prove to be mere illusions.

As a government official, Spenser was involved in England's attempts at erecting permanent "monuments" on Irish soil in the shape of the accomplishment of its conquest and the establishment of English civility. But his poetry suggests that no intervention, whether armed or not, has so far been decisive, no achievement durable. It does so in the fictional representation of the difficulty of establishing permanent English rule over Ireland: Artegall is recalled to Faerie Court before he can thoroughly "reforme" and "redresse" Irena's reign (*FQ* 5.12.27). Irena herself is left in "heauiness" (st. 27) and Artegall returns "halfe sad / From his late conquest" (6.1.4): Grantorto is defeated, but Irena's rule and control over the country are not secure, therefore any other "giant" can suddenly destroy again all that has been rebuilt. The Arlo Hill myth (7.6) furthers the view that no human effort can restore the place to its prelapsarian beauty.

The paradoxical impulse to monumentalize and at the same time to characterize all monuments as impermanent is everywhere apparent in Spenser's work. *The Faerie Queene* is a monument to the effort and skill needed to produce an epic meant to contribute to the shaping of a national identity, and to the mythologization of the English empire

IV The Sight of Ruins and the "Sabaoths Sight"   153

through a careful recording of England's part historical, part legendary past and optimistic predictions of future glory. The same person who erects that literary monument to England that is *The Faerie Queene* has reflected since early youth (as his correspondence with Gabriel Harvey and his early translations from Du Bellay attest) upon the fact that mutability's absolute sway over the world makes all human endeavours vain. *Ruines of Time*, written in the same period as he was raising an imperial shrine in the *Faerie Queene*, examines the greatest empires and civilizations of the past and insists on the fact that nothing of them is left save wasted stones.[194]

The account of the fall of Rome in *The Visions of Bellay*, Spenser's translation of Du Bellay's *Antiquitez de Rome*, serves to show that empires built by mortals in order to impose a human kind of order on other mortals share the mortal character of their founders, hence harbour the seed of corruption and transience. Monuments sooner or later turn to dust and with them vanishes the memory of the mundane glory and power they represented. History teaches that "Princes pallaces fell fast / To ruine: (for what thing can euer last?)" (*Mother Hubberds Tale* 1175). But not just monuments and empires are swept away. Their clients and founders face the same destiny. Even the greatest, most virtuous or powerful, share "mans wretched state, / That floures so fresh at morne, and fades at euening late," as Britomart comments with regard to the "Troians bold" wiped out by the Greeks (3.9.39, 38).

In *Ruines of Time*, Spenser's eulogy of dead members of the Sidney, Dudley and Russell families is set against the background of a broader reflection upon the futility of human endeavours. Leicester and Sidney's association with Protestant imperial ambitions is suddenly broken off by death. Everything is left unfinished, imperfect, incomplete.

---

[194] "Although the poem may contain sections of early material, particularly in the first of the emblematic sequences, the allusion to the death of Walsingham indicates that the text was revised as late as 6 April 1590 (435-41)" (McCabe, *Shorter Poems* 584).

"I saw him die": the repetition, three times in two lines (190, 193), of Verlame's dismayed exclamation, gives the idea of her shock at the end of a man, Leicester, in whom so many hopes were invested. Since now that he is dead "all is with him dead" (211), it is clear that not even Leicester, for all his "glorie" and "greatnes" (218, 219), could leave something durable behind. And this of course is yet another demonstration of the evanescence of all that is human and earthly. Sidney's sudden end is another exemplum of transience likely to impress Spenser's contemporary readers more deeply than the fall of some great emperor of the past, because of its proximity in space and time. Sidney, Verlame laments, who was exceptionally gifted in so many ways, possessing a "treasure passing all this worldes worth" (286), constantly engaging for "his countries good" (301), is now in "*Elisian* fields" (332), carried off "too soone" (291) by death, where "too soone" in my view expresses both the regret for his untimely death, and also the idea that he went before he could complete the erection of the patriotic and poetic "monuments" expected from him.

Reflection upon the fact that not even an empire like the Roman could successfully defy time and change, that not even a Sidney or a Leicester could complete their "monuments" or make them durable suggests that literary creations, the fruits of mortal intellects, are equally ephemeral. *Ruines of Time* questions the humanistic belief in the eternizing power of poetry which is expressed by Verlame, whose earthly perspective, I argue, is to some extent discredited by the Christian context of the poem.[195] From the perspective of heaven that the second vision represents, all mortal efforts are rendered inadequate and imperfect. It is very typical of the often contradictory and paradoxical nature of Spenser's art that he suggests poetry, the product of

---

[195] In his edition of *Complaints*, W. L. Renwick lists the chief classical sources of the theme of immortality through poetry: "Horace's *Odes*, III.xxx, IV.viii and ix; Ovid, *Amores*, I.xv, *Metamorphoses* xv, 871; and *Propertius*, III; Theocritus, *Idyll* xvi" (196). Renwick argues that the theme of poetic immortality is "inevitable in an elegy on a poet," hence its presence in *Ruines of Time* (190).

IV The Sight of Ruins and the "Sabaoths Sight" 155

mortal wit, cannot create anything immortal or bestow immortality on its objects, in a work "intended [. . .] to the eternizing of [. . .] late deceased" personalities variously related to the Countess of Pembroke (*Ruines of Time*, dedication).

The tension between the impulse to create permanent poetic structures that impose a temporal, physical or numerological order upon the magmatic world and the realization of the fragility of this order that is as easily dissolved as the ring of perfection of the dancing Graces is pervasive throughout Spenser's work. As a poet, Spenser claims his task is to create something "that steel in strength, and time in durance shall outweare" (*Shepheardes Calender*, envoy) and to erect "immortall moniment[s]" (*Amoretti* 69.10) to human achievements. As a Christian, however, he knows that eternity is God's. *Ruines of Time* subverts the hubris in the humanist idea that poetry is immune from the limitations inherent in any other human endeavour. Verulame, as a spokeswoman of the humanist view, argues at length that the "*Muses*" "vnto men eternitie do giue" (366, 367), setting them free "from bands of implacable fate, / And power of death" (395, 396). Ironically, however, the Muses themselves, *Teares of the Muses* suggest, are forgotten. Verlame's is a very secular idea of transcendence and survival through literary works and in the memory of future generations. But those, she fails to consider, share the imperfection and vanity she so meticulously has shown are the character of all that is human and earthly.

The perspective of immortality through poetry that Verlame promotes is clearly inadequately comforting and she ends her "piteous plaint, / With dolefull shrikes" (470-71). Nothing can console the "worldlings" for the impermanence and imperfection of human monuments. Sympathetic towards "that same womans piteous paine" (480), the narrator at first adopts the same earthly perspectives, renews "her complaint with passion strong" and is equally left "greeuing" (479, 484). His inconsolable melancholy signals his lack of spiritual perspectives. The narrator tries to see the purpose and meaning behind the state of things on earth that Verulame has described so well. He strives "to wreste" the "meaning" of her "speach" (486, 485), but finds it is out of his "slender reasons reach" (487); the meaning and direction of human history can be grasped only through "visions" recorded as enigmas and signs by the poet. And in fact the narrator is granted two series of visions: the first confirms that any mortal endeavour is but "vanitie and griefe of minde" (583). The other confirms that what is mortal can at best be perpetual but not eternal, permanence is only beyond this world, and "hope of heauen" is the only "comfort" (585, 584). It is the "drosse of sinfull worlds *desire*" (686; emphasis mine), not the world itself that the Christian must shun. Calvin says that "to believers the whole earth is blessed" (1: 403); it is blessed and transitional, hence loathing of it and immoderate attachment to it are equally false attitudes.

If this life is only provisional, so is everything humans produce in the course of their life including literary works and the survival in memory they offer. In fact Spenser's narrators, characters and poetic personae observe throughout his work that nothing can be completed on earth, nothing can get close to that perfection, fulfilment, permanence that exist only beyond the corrupt and mortal. Human creations, whether material, political, philosophical, literary, share the nature of the imperfect created world and are equally subject to the great cycle of change, decay, death. Spenser's work thematizes the idea that, necessarily, all humans take in hand to achieve is an "endlesse worke" (*FQ* 4.12.1) that will never be finished. In this light, *The Faerie Queene* is a paradigmatical representation of the world as the reign of incompleteness; one has just to consider "how many of the stories are incomplete, how few of the poem's lovers are united, how the achievement of each major quest is in some sense qualified" (Campbell 50). Rather than the product of some failure of inspiration or artistic insufficiency on Spenser's part, this appears as a dramatization of the view that the "ultimate conclusion lies beyond the human" (50).

IV The Sight of Ruins and the "Sabaoths Sight"   157

By reflecting in what may have been intended as a coda to his epic, the *Cantos*, on the workings of mutability, and by comparing mortal life as it appears to the eyes of the flesh with the immortality "revealed" in "visions" obtained through faith, Spenser's narrator expresses the Christian view that fulfilment lies not in the course of mortal life, but beyond. With regard to one of the many stories in *The Faerie Queene* wanting an end, Marinell's narrative, Spenser's narrator announces, "to another place I leaue to be perfected" (4.12.35): but there is no other place in the poem where this story will be given an end. As the reader has learned from *Complaints*, as from other Spenserian works, human artifacts have no real conclusion, no sense of completion in the here and now. This state of affairs, Spenser's texts again and again show, bewilders and saddens humans on whom mutability plays "her cruell sports" (7.6.1).

158 Paola Baseotto

13. Perspectives on Mutabilitie

In my view, consideration of two peculiarities of the *Mutabilitie Cantos*, one formal, the other narrational, is crucial for an understanding of their meaning and function. The form of the *Cantos* is extremely significant: they appear to be a fragment of an unfinished book. Their incompleteness serves as an emblem of abortive human effort and points to the idea that one has to look beyond the human and earthly for conclusions and answers.

The incomplete *Cantos* seem to provide a kind of conclusion to the incomplete *Faerie Queene*. They end with two stanzas of an "unperfite" canto (*FQ* 7.8, heading) in the voice of Spenser's narrator. In the first he expresses his disappointment and distress, his loathing of reality as it appears to him; in the second he voices the hope that the reality of mortal life can be finally and utterly changed, and that beyond the human lies a dimension where everything will eventually turn into its opposite, mortality into immortality, change into permanence, loss into gain. Since he cannot describe what he does not know, what has not yet come about, it is appropriate that the *Cantos* be left unfinished, with the narrator writing about his wish. God is left to bring both Spenser's narrator's personal story and the long story of the world to an end, by granting him the "Sabaoths sight" soon, and the world, one day, "stedfast rest" (7.8.2).

Another peculiarity of the *Mutabilitie Cantos* that in my view is crucial for their interpretation, in terms of the presentation of people as sufferers that I have analyzed in the present study, is the apparent transformation Mutabilitie undergoes as the narrative progresses. This is not a physical transformation: Mutabilitie is not a shape-shifting deity like Proteus or a living deceit like Duessa. Mutabilitie exemplifies a recurring theme in Spenser's work that things and persons can be seen in different lights, can seem different to observers whose points of view are different. In fact Spenser gives us various perceptions of Mutabilitie's features and personality, and makes it clear that she does not seem to be perceived consistently, appearing to some as unpleas-

IV The Sight of Ruins and the "Sabaoths Sight" 159

ant and rough, to others as beautiful and dignified.[196] I shall argue that this at the same time reiterates the characteristic Spenserian theme of the limits of fleshly views, and suggests that those who see and judge her are not entirely responsible for their short-sightedness.

When portrayed within the sphere of the moon, Mutabilitie is described in terms of her faults and is blamed for a number of misdeeds. She belongs to the "bad seed" of the Titans and is "fraught with pride and impudence" (7.6.21, 25); she plays "cruell sports, to many mens decay" (st. 1); she has broken the laws of "Nature," "Iustice," "Policie" and has "death for life exchanged foolishlie" (st. 6). However, when she rises above the sublunar sphere and appears before the assembly of gods presided over by Jove, her charms are revealed: the gods notice her "grace," her "stature tall" and how "beautifull of face" she is (7.6.28). When he looks on her "louely face, / In which, faire beames of beauty did appeare," Jove, who meant to "thunder-driue" her to hell (7.6.31, 30), refrains from doing so. If, as Pauline Parker has argued (262-63), evil in Spenser is always ugly and deformed, even if that ugliness is sometimes masked, while the outward beauty of the vertuous is a sign of their inner goodness, then Mutabilitie's real and great fairness would seem to be a sign of her being ultimately good. In my view, the fact that Mutabilitie's beauty is visible only above the sublunary sphere is crucial to the themes of the *Cantos* and offers a useful key to the interpretation of the narrator's final prayer.

In the *Cantos* the reader is presented with the clearest exemplification of the idea that I have traced through Spenser's work, of the conflict between fleshly and spiritual perspectives. This idea to a great extent generates the tensions and contradictions that are discernible in the *Cantos*. It produces references to four different planes, the human, the natural, the cosmic, the divine. Everything is seen either in its en-

---

[196] Most commentators on the *Cantos* make reference to Mutabilitie's appearance, although in perspectives that are different from mine. An interesting view is found in Berleth's article "Fraile Woman, Foolish Gerle: Misogyny in Spenser's Mutabilitie Cantos."

tirety or partiality and presents a different aspect depending on the position of the observer, hence everything seems different to observers placed on different planes. The case of Mutabilitie is paradigmatical: from the earthly point of view she seems ugly and violent, from the natural, useful and ultimately beneficial if also cruel; from the cosmic, beautiful, from the divine, providential. Clearly, from a Christian point of view, it is only from the divine perspective that things can be seen in their entirety and true essence.

The point is that unfortunately, as Spenser's texts again and again insist, people cannot but see things from the earthly perspective; at best when they see a "vision," viz when they hold on to the perspectives of faith, they have a glimpse of the truth, they get an idea, however vague, of what things really look like. The providential plan whose agent is mutability is largely invisible to human eyes. A Redcrosse, a Britomart, a Guyon can only see the accidents of their lives as purposeful steps towards a God-guided goal when a Contemplation, or a Merlin, or some "antique Registers" (*FQ* 2.9.59) point out the providential movement that regulates the apparent chaotic flux of change. Normally, what people know of Mutabilitie is what they "plainly feele," that the "euer-whirling wheele / Of *Change* [. . .] all mortall things doth sway," and that Mutabilitie plays "her cruell sports, to many mens decay" (7.6.1). To humans, Mutabilitie is principally responsible for the general process of decay and degeneration that sways everything and everybody and that Spenser's narrator so often laments.

What Spenser's characters and speakers experience is the suffering arising from the series of losses change brings about. Their perception of reality is represented as limited in space and time and thus what they notice of mutability's activity are its effects on single individual lives, not on life generally in the universe. In the *Cantos*, on the contrary, the visionary narrative allows the reader to see mutability from the perspective of Nature and that of the gods assembled on Arlo

IV The Sight of Ruins and the "Sabaoths Sight" 161

Hill.[197] It is only from this perspective that the pageant of "times and seasons" (7.7.27) presents itself in its entirety; only from this perspective can we see that Nature's sergeant, Order, keeps everything in rank, producing the fertility of creation.

The only chance sublunary mortals have to glimpse what is usually invisible to human eyes is when philosophy and faith broaden a little the human narrow field of vision. The narrative technique of the *Cantos* is a myth about an illuminating journey of explanation about the mystery of earthly life with philosophy, faith and medieval tradition as guides. This explanation is beyond doubt optimistic; Spenser's narrator gives us a vision which presents the providential hand of God at work in the apparent disorder of the world. But this vision does not alter his pessimistic outlook on human affairs, because a universal perspective does not console him for his sense of personal loss, nor does the promise of an Edenic destination make the journey seem less exhausting. In this chapter, my aim is to show how crucial the different perspectives, human, natural, cosmic, and divine, of the *Cantos* prove to be for its vision narrative of the laws governing earthly life.

The view of mortal life as unified, but differently understood from different perspectives, accounts to a great extent for the tension one perceives throughout the *Cantos* between optimistic argument and melancholic pessimism. Mutability may ultimately be the creative force driving the universe, but to people it appears as a destructive power, a bringer of decay, death, loss, hence suffering, to individuals. People see the havoc change and time make of their life and even when they are aware that the cycle of life and death is part of a great process of perpetual regeneration, they feel it is cruel that destruction must be the means through which perpetuation is achieved. From their

---

[197] On the complex issue of the simultaneous representation of Jove as a "planetary god," whose perspective is therefore cosmic, as well as a spokesman of God himself, and of Nature's superhuman status as a symbol of "God's creative power," see Sheldon P. Zitner's introduction in his excellent edition of *The Mutabilitie Cantos* (52, 49).

limited point of view, they see things more or less as Mutabilitie herself does, they observe that "new creatures [. . .] arize" out of the "decay and mortall crime" (7.7.18) of other creatures. They quite naturally incline to loath this life that feeds on death. An effective exemplification of this fact is the episode of the darkening of the earth when Mutabilitie contends with Cynthia, the moon. People ignore the cause of this phenomenon, all they see is darkness "the lower World [. . .] nothing knew / Of all that chaunced here" (7.6.14). "Griesly shadowes" often cover "heauen bright" and make it impossible for human eyes to see its "thousand starres" (3.4.52).

However, the witnesses Mutabilitie calls when she pleads her case before Nature and the gods, that is, the pageant of the months and seasons, contradict rather than confirm her declaration that everything is caught in an aimless, disorderly circular process of change, decay, death, rebirth. In fact, the pageant proves there is order in the universe; within it change and death are part of a universal process progressing along a linear, not circular path directed to the "perfection" (7.7.58), not the destruction of things. "All things," as Nature states in her verdict, "by their change their being doe dilate" (7.7.58); progress, not a chaotic movement towards corruption, is discernible in the universe. Life and death are clearly part of a continuous natural process of regeneration through change. Mutability, therefore, which may seem an agent of destruction, is also and above all a creative and conservative force. Mutabilitie's nature and function as they manifest themselves on the natural plane are thus defined. But on a higher plane, in the divine perspective, it is clear that permanence in flux and the conservation of everything as it is, is not the ultimate aim towards which all things proceed led by Mutabilitie: beyond mere conservation and continuation lie evolution and progress towards higher ends.

Sherman Hawkins has stressed how the cycle of the months was traditionally seen as pointing to the work of Providence in the universe, as evidence of God's plan for it (88, 90). The cycle epitomizes the promise of redemption as it begins in March, the month the Incarna-

IV The Sight of Ruins and the "Sabaoths Sight"   163

tion was announced. Besides, Nature's final verdict attests to Spenser's appropriation of Boethian views of a God-guided universal movement. Her argument is that although things do change, they do so not fortuitously, since in reality they are "rightly wayd" and "worke their owne perfection so by fate" (7.7.58). The will and fate that Nature describes as governing earthly change are clearly one with Boethius's Providence and Fate:

> Providence is the divine reason itself which belongs to the most high ruler of all things and which governs all things; Fate, however, belongs to all mutable things and is the disposition by which Providence joins all things in their own order. [. . .] This Providence is the unfolding of temporal events even as this is present to the vision of the divine mind; but this same unfolding of events as it is worked out in time is called Fate. (91)[198]

All things progress towards their own "perfection" (7.7.58) (Latin *perficere* 'to accomplish'), that is their end, the moment when "all shall changed bee, / And from thenceforth, none no more change shall see" (st. 59). So Mutabilitie leads things to a death that is a birth, she leads people and things back into God's lap through death. From this perspective, Mutabilitie appears beautiful. Far from being the evil power mortal sufferers deem her to be, she holds a very important place in God's providential scheme. As an agent of his plan, she completes creation and leads everything to eternity.

Many Spenserian characters share Alcyon's view of a world endlessly turning "like a Mill wheele, in midst of miserie, / Driuen with streames of wretchednesse and woe" (*Daphnaida* 432-33). The world does turn as a "Mill wheele," but it is "driuen" by human misery; sorrow is the price individuals have to pay to contribute to the continua-

---

[198] Lipsius defines Providence as "an absolute and perfect knowledge of the celestiall God: which hath two faculties neerlie allied unto it, Necessitie and Destinie" (114).

tion of universal life. It is a price that in Spenser's texts no one pays willingly, least of all the narrator for whom the vision of Mutabilitie

> Makes [him] loath this state of life so tickle,
> And loue of things so vaine to cast away;
> Whose flowring pride, so fading and so fickle,
> Short Time shall soon cut down with his consuming sickle.
>
> *(FQ* 7.8.1)

But to resist the flux of change, to withdraw from life in order to avoid pain is to immure oneself in a living death, as such Spenserian narratives as Marinell's show (*FQ* 3.4). While suffering leads those who hold fleshly perspectives to inconsolable despair, those who view things with the eye of the spirit are led to a prayer. The instability, transience, and changefulness of earthly things arouse in the narrator an intense desire for the end of all desires.[199] The prayer that concludes the *Cantos* orthodoxly submits the desire for "no more Change" and "stedfast rest" to the will of "that great Sabbaoth God" (7.8.2).

In a sense, the complaint of the penultimate stanza of the *Cantos* echoes all the complaints Spenserian sufferers express throughout his work, but it also transcends them. If the narrator's final appeal to God is the expression of a death-wish, unlike those of other Spenserian sufferers it arises more from hope than despair. His is not just a desire of death out of exhaustion and impatience, or the fury of Alcyon who declares he hates the world and would like to see it transformed into a wasteland (*Daphnaida* 393-434, 330-50). It is the desire of one who has been granted a "vision," one who has been shown by philosophy and faith that the state of things on earth is not meaninglessly cruel,

---

[199] "Desire implies lack, hence imperfection. To be eternal and hence non-mutable is also to be free of desire. Conversely to be human is to be mutable and to desire. So the absolute object of desire is, experientially, a fantasy of the *absolute release from desire*, i.e., death of desire/death of self" (Dollimore, "Desire is Death" 375).

IV The Sight of Ruins and the "Sabaoths Sight" 165

but that there is order, aim, reason behind events. Divine Providence is at work, but it is at work in a world that is postlapsarian, hence marked by corruption and the limitations of mortality. His wish reveals his longing for something better and is not just a desire of release from the pains and toils of life. It is a longing for the beginning of something, not just for the end of something else.

The "vision" of Spenser's narrator, however, does not make the evils of life disappear from his view. If the episode of Mutabilitie suggests that the state of earthly affairs is necessary and part of a Providential plan, it also underlines that neither purpose, nor meaning make human suffering vanish. Besides, the *Cantos* show how little is visible from the immediate earthly perspective and how even that little appears deformed, like Mutabilitie. Boethius may have described the visitation of Philosophy, and Spenser's narrator is carried "too high flight, vnfit for her weake wing" (7.7.1) by his Muse, but as in *Ruines of Time*, visions are narrated by mortals and inextricably partake of mortal art and mortal perspectives. They give no direct access to the invisible "Sabbaoth God" that is beyond mortal sight.

The *Cantos* suggest that while people should accept the status quo as necessary and purposeful, they cannot be expected to do so enthusiastically or get used to loving this "state of life so tickle" (7.8.1). Spenser dramatizes with sympathy his death-wishers' and sufferers' view: life is indeed painful, God's "heauy haplesse curse" (7.6.55) on humanity and the world has made it so. Nature's verdict, that Mutabilitie is necessary in this world for its ultimate good and hence must continue to work until she will die at the end of time, means that people will always suffer losses, see their loved ones die, see their efforts thwarted and their "monuments" ruined. Even after revelation through the agency of his Muse that individual lives have a meaning and a place in God's plan, the narrator longs not to have this life prolonged, but to leave it, to transcend it through death. He asks God to grant him the "Sabaoths sight" (7.8.2); he longs to see things finally transfigured, snatched from mortality, transferred from Mutabilitie's deadly to God's loving embrace.

As so often elsewhere in Spenser's texts, death is seen as the greatest good and the intense longing for it the reader perceives throughout Spenser's work is finally expressed openly and given fuller meaning. To death is entrusted the most crucial of all quests: to annihilate human suffering, imperfection and impermanence whose mystery in the end is not unravelled, but cancelled in death. It is up to death to finish Spenser's unfinished poem in a language no mortal can ever read and the epilogue is an anticipation of his encounter with the "great Sabbaoth God."

Bibliography

Editions of Spenser's works, the Bible, and Shakespeare's works used in this study are listed in "Note on texts" on page xii.

– Primary Sources

Abbot, George. *An Exposition upon the Prophet Jonah*. 1600. London: Hamilton, Adams & Co., 1845.

Aquinas, Saint Thomas. *The Summa Theologica*. Trans. Father Laurence Shapcote. Great Books of the Western World 17 and 18. 2 vols. Chicago: Encyclopaedia Britannica, 1952.

Augustine. *The City of God*. Trans. John Healey. Everyman's Library 982 and 983. 2 vols. London: Dent & Sons, 1945.

Batman, Stephen. *The Doome warning all Men to the Judgemente: Wherein are contayned for the most parte all the straunge Prodiges hapned in the Worlde, with divers secrete figures of Revelations tending to mannes stayed conversion towardes God: In maner of a generall Chronicle, gathered out of sundrie approved authors by St. Batman professor in Divinitie*. 1581. Delmar, N.Y.: Scholar's Facsimile Reprints, 1984.

Becon, Thomas. *The Dialogue between the Christian Knight and Satan, wherein Satan moveth unto Desperation, the Knight comforteth himself with the sweet promises of the Holy Scripture. A Catechism*. 1577. By Becon. Cambridge: Parker Society, 1844.

___. *The Jewel of ioy. A Catechism*. 1577. By Becon. Cambridge: Parker Society, 1844.

___. *The Sicke Mannes Salue, Wherein the faithfull Christians may learne both how to behaue themselues patiently and thankefully in the tyme of sickenes, and also vertuously to dispose their temporall goods, and finally to prepare themselues gladly and godly to dye*. 1560. *Prayers and Other Pieces*. By Becon. Cambridge: Parker Society, 1844.

___. *The Solace of the Soule, veri comfortable against the bytter stormes of sicknes and death, greatly encouragyng the faythful both paciently and thanckefully to suffer the good pleasure of God in all kynde of aduersytye.* 1548. *A Catechism.* By Becon. 1577. Cambridge: Parker Society, 1844.

Boethius. *The Consolation of Philosophy.* 524. Trans. Richard Green. New York: Macmillan, 1987.

Bradford, John. *Sermons and Meditations.* Cambridge: Parker Society, 1848.

Burton, Robert. *The Anatomy of Melancholy.* 1621. Ed. Thomas C. Faulkner, Nicolas K. Kiessling, and Rhonda L. Blair. 3 vols. Oxford: Clarendon Press, 1989-.

Calvin, John. *Institutes of the Christian Religion.* Ed. T. McNeill. Trans. Ford Lewis Battles. Library of Christian Classics 20 and 21. 2 vols. London: S.C.M., 1961.

Catullus. *Catullus Tibullus and Pervigilium Veneris.* Trans. F. W. Cornish. Loeb Classical Library. London: Heinemann, 1950.

Chapman, George. *The Conspiracy and Tragedy of Charles, Duke of Byron.* 1608. Ed. George Ray. 2 vols. New York: Garland, 1979.

Chaucer, Geoffrey. *The Canterbury Tales.* Ed. Larry D. Benson. The Riverside Chaucer. Oxford: Oxford University Press, 1987.

Cicero, Marcus Tullius. *The Tusculan Questions.* Trans. George A. Otis. Boston: James B. Dow, 1839.

Coverdale, Myles. "Treatise on Death." *Remains.* Cambridge: Parker Society, 1846.

Erasmus, Desiderius. *Preparation to Deathe.* 1538. Amsterdam: Theatrum Orbis Terrarum, 1975, a facsimile reproduction.

___. "A treatise perswadyng a man patiently to suffer the death of his freend." 1550. *A comfortable exhortacion agaynst the chaunces of death.* London: Thomas Berthelet, 1553.

Gardner, Helen, ed. *The New Oxford Book of English Verse, 1250-1950.* Oxford: Clarendon Press, 1972.

Horace. *The Odes and Epodes.* Trans. C. E. Bennett. Loeb Classical Library. London: Heinemann, 1914.

Kierkegaard, Søren. *The Sickness Unto Death: A Christian Psychological Exposition for Upbuilding and Awakening.* Ed. and trans. Howard V. Hong and Edna H. Hong. Princeton: Princeton University Press, 1980.

Latimer, Hugh. "Sermons and Remains." *Works.* By Latimer. Cambridge: Parker Society, 1844.

Lipsius, Iustus. *Two Bookes of Constancie.* 1584. Trans. Sir John Stradling. 1594. Ed. Rudolf Kirk. New Brunswick, N. J.: Rutgers University Press, 1939.

Mornay, Philippe du Plessis. *A discovrse of life and death. Written in French by Phil. Mornay. Done in English by the Countesse of Pembroke.* London: William Ponsonby, 1600.

Noot, Jan van Der. *A Theatre wherein be represented as wel the Miseries and Calamities that follow the Voluptuous Worldlings, as also the Greate Ioyes and Plesures which the Faithfull do Enioy (1569).* Spenser, *Variorum.* Vol. 8.

Osborn, James M., ed. *The Autobiography of Thomas Whythorne.* London: Oxford University Press, 1962.

Perkins, William. *A Salve for a Sicke Man or, A Treatise Containing the Nature, Differences, and Kindes of Death; as Also the Right Manner of Dying Well.* 1595. *The works of that famovs and worthy Minister of Christ in the Vniversitie of Cambridge.* 3 vols. London: Iohn Legatt, 1631. Vol. 1.

___. *The Whole Treatise of the Cases of Conscience.* 1606. *The works of that famovs and worthy Minister of Christ in the Vniversitie of Cambridge.* Vol. 2.

Seneca. *Letters to Lucilius.* Trans. E. Phillips Barker. 2 vols. Oxford: Clarendon Press, 1932.

Skelton, John. *Magnificence.* 1530. Ed. Paula Neuss. Manchester: Manchester University Press, 1980.

Southwell, Robert. "Upon the Image of Death." *The New Oxford Book of English Verse, 1250-1950*. Ed. Helen Gardner. Oxford: Clarendon Press, 1972.

Strode, George. *The Anatomie of Mortalitie*. London: William Iones, 1618.

Sym, John. *Lifes Preservative against Self-killing or An Vseful Treatise Concerning Life and Self-murder*. London: M. Flesher, 1637.

Whythorne, Thomas. See Osborn, James M.

Thomas Wright. *The Passions of the Minde*. London: V. S[immes], 1601.

– **Secondary Sources**

Allen, Don Cameron. "The Degeneration of Man and Renaissance Pessimism." *Studies in Philology* 35 (1938): 202-27.

Anderson, Ruth L. *Elizabethan Psychology and Shakespeare's Plays*. Iowa City: University of Iowa Press, 1927.

Ariès, Philippe. *The Hour of Our Death*. Trans. Helen Weaver. New York: Random House, 1982.

___. *Western Attitudes toward Death*. Trans. Patricia M. Ranum. Baltimore: Johns Hopkins University Press, 1974.

Babb, Lawrence. *The Elizabethan Malady: A Study of Melancholia in English Literature from 1580 to 1642*. East Lansing, Mich.: Michigan State University Press, 1951.

Baseotto, Paola. "Godly Sorrow, Damnable Despair and *Faerie Queene* I.ix." *Cahiers Elisabéthains* 69 (2006): 1-11.

Beaty, Nancy Lee. *The Craft of Dying: A Study in the Literary Tradition of the Ars Moriendi in England*. Yale Studies in English 175. New Haven: Yale University Press, 1970.

Beecher, Donald A. "The Anatomy of Melancholy in Book I of the *Faerie Queene*." *Renaissance and Reformation* 24.2 (1988): 85-99.

———. "Spenser's Redcrosse Knight and his Encounter with Despair: Some Aspects of the 'Elizabethan Malady.'" *Renaissance and Reformation* 11.1 (1987): 1-15.

Bellamy, Jane, Patrick Cheney, and Michael Schoenfeldt, eds. *Imagining Death in Spenser and Milton.* London: Palgrave Macmillan, 2004.

Berger, Harry, Jr. *Revisionary Play: Studies in the Spenserian Dynamics.* Berkeley and Los Angeles: University of California Press, 1988.

Berleth, Richard J. "Fraile Woman, Foolish Gerle: Misogyny in Spenser's Mutabilitie Cantos." *Modern Philology* 1 (1995): 37-53.

Bultmann, Rudolf C. Life and Death. Trans. P. H. Ballard and D. Turner. Ed. P. R. Ackroyd. London: Adam & Charles Black, 1965.

Bultot, Robert. *La doctrine du mépris du monde en Occident, de Saint Ambroise à Innocent III.* Louvain: Nauwelaerts, 1964.

Campbell, Marion. "Spenser's *Mutabilitie Cantos* and the End of *The Faerie Queene.*" *Southern Review* 1 (1982): 46-59.

Cheney, Donald. "Dido to Daphne: Early Modern Death in Spenser's Shorter Poems." *Spenser Studies* 18 (2003): 143-63.

———. "Spenser's Fortieth Birthday and Related Fictions." *Spenser Studies* 4 (1983): 3-31.

———. *Spenser's Image of Nature: Wild Man and Shepherd in 'The Faerie Queene.'* New Haven: Yale University Press, 1966.

Cherniss, Michael D. *Boethian Apocalypse: Studies in Middle English Vision Poetry.* Norman, Okla.: Pilgrim, 1987.

Crampton, Georgia Ronan. *The Condition of Creatures: Suffering and Action in Chaucer and Spenser.* New Haven and London: Yale University Press, 1974.

Cressy, David. *Birth, Marriage, and Death: Ritual, Religion and the Life-Cycle in Tudor and Stuart England.* Oxford: Oxford University Press, 1997.

Dietrich, Bernard C. *Death, Fate and the Gods: The Development of a Religious Idea in Greek Popular Belief and in Homer*. London: Athlone, 1967.

Dixon, Michael F. N. *The Polliticke Courtier: Spenser's 'The Faerie Queene' as a Rhetoric of Justice*. Montreal and Kingston: McGill-Queen's University Press, 1996.

Dollimore, Jonathan. *Death, Desire and Loss in Western Culture*. London: Allen Lane, Penguin, 1998.

——. "Desire is Death." Grazia, Quilligan, and Stallybrass, eds., 369-86.

Durston, Christopher, and Jacqueline Eales, eds. *The Culture of English Puritanism, 1560-1700*. London: Macmillan, 1996.

Enright, Dennis J. *The Oxford Book of Death*. Oxford: Oxford University Press, 1983.

Escobedo, Andrew. "Despair and the Proportion of the Self." *Spenser Studies* 18 (2003): 75-90.

Foucault, Michel. *The Order of Things: An Archeology of the Human Sciences*. London: Routledge, 2001.

Fowler, Alastair D. S. "The Image of Mortality: The Faerie Queene II.i-ii." *Essential Articles for the Study of Edmund Spenser*. Ed. A. C. Hamilton.

Garland, Robert. *The Greek Way of Death*. London: Duckworth, 1985.

A General Index to the Publications of the Parker Society. Comp. Henry Gough. Cambridge: Parker Society, 1855.

Gittings, Clare. *Death, Burial and the Individual in Early Modern England*. London: Croom Helm, 1984.

Gordon, Bruce, and Peter Marshall. *The Place of Death: Death and Remembrance in Late Medieval and Early Modern Europe*. Cambridge: Cambridge University Press, 2000.

Grant, Patrick. *Images and Ideas in Literature of the English Renaissance*. London: Macmillan, 1979.

Grazia, Margreta de, Maureen Quilligan, and Peter Stallybrass, eds. *Subject and Object in Renaissance Culture*. Cambridge Studies in

Renaissance Literature and Culture 8. Cambridge: Cambridge University Press, 1996.
Hadfield, Andrew, ed. *Edmund Spenser*. Longman Critical Readers. London: Longman, 1996.
Hamilton, A. C., ed. *Essential Articles for the Study of Edmund Spenser*. Hamden, Conn.: Archon Books, 1972.
___. Donald Cheney, David A. Richardson, and William W. Barker, eds. *The Spenser Encyclopedia*. Toronto, Buffalo and London: University of Toronto Press, 1990.
___. *The Structure of Allegory in 'The Faerie Queene.'* Oxford: Clarendon Press, 1961.
Hankins, John Erskine. *Source and Meaning in Spenser's Allegory: A Study of 'The Faerie Queene.'* Oxford: Clarendon Press, 1971.
Harris, Duncan and Nancy L. Steffen. "The Other Side of the Garden: An Interpretative Comparison of Chaucer's *Book of the Duchess* and Spenser's *Daphnaida*." *Journal of Medieval and Renaissance Studies* 8 (1978): 17-36.
Harris, Victor. *All Coherence Gone*. Chicago, Ill.: University of Chicago Press, 1949.
Hawkins, Sherman. "Mutability and the Cycle of the Months." *Form and Convention in the Poetry of Edmund Spenser*. Ed. William Nelson.
Hazard, Mark. "The Other Apocalypse: Spenser's Use of 2 Esdras in the Book of Justice." *Spenser Studies* 14 (2000): 163-87.
Heale, Elizabeth. *The Faerie Queene: A Reader's Guide*. 2nd ed. Cambridge: Cambridge University Press, 1999.
Hoeniger, David F. *Medicine and Shakespeare in the English Renaissance*. Newark, Del.: University of Delaware Press, 1992.
___. "Aesculapius." *Spenser Encyclopedia*. Ed A. C. Hamilton et al.
Houlbrooke, Ralph A. *Death, Religion, and the Family in England, 1480-1750*. Oxford: Clarendon Press, 1998.

___. "The Puritan Death-bed, c. 1560 - c. 1660." *The Culture of English Puritanism, 1560-1700*. Ed. Christopher Durston and Jacqueline Eales. 122-44.

Howard, Donald R. "Renaissance World-Alienation." *The Darker Vision of the Renaissance*. Ed. Robert Kinsman. 47-77.

Hume, Anthea. *Edmund Spenser: Protestant Poet*. Cambridge: Cambridge University Press, 1984.

Hyde, Thomas. "Vision." *Spenser Encyclopedia*. Ed A. C. Hamilton et al.

Kay, Dennis. *Melodious Tears: The English Funeral Elegy from Spenser to Milton*. Oxford: Clarendon Press, 1990.

Kerrigan, John, ed. *Motives of Woe: Shakespeare and 'Female Complaint': A Critical Anthology*. Oxford: Clarendon Press, 1991.

Kinsman, Robert S., ed. *The Darker Vision of the Renaissance*. Berkeley: University of California Press, 1974.

Koller, Kathrine. "Art, Rhetoric, and Holy Dying in the *Faerie Queene* with Special Reference to the Despair Canto." *Studies in Philology* 61 (1964): 128-39.

Kristeva, Julia. *Soleil noir: Dépression et mélancolie*. Paris: Gallimard, 1987.

___. *Pouvoirs de l'horreur. Essai sur l'abjection*. Paris: Seuil, 1980.

Lambert, Ellen Z. "Elegy, pastoral." *Spenser Encyclopedia*. Ed A. C. Hamilton et al.

___. *Placing Sorrow: A Study of the Pastoral Elegy Convention from Theocritus to Milton*. Chapel Hill: University of North Carolina Press, 1976.

Laurent, Alain. *Histoire de l'individualisme*. Paris: PUF, 1993.

Leslie, Michael. *Spenser's 'Fierce Warres and Faithfull Loves': Martial and Chivalric Symbolism in 'The Faerie Queene.'* Cambridge: Brewer, 1983.

Lewis, C. S. *English Literature in the Sixteenth Century Excluding Drama*. Oxford: Clarendon Press, 1954.

Lyons, Bridget Gellert. *Voices of Melancholy: Studies in Literary Treatments of Melancholy in Renaissance England*. London: Routledge, 1971.
MacDonald, Michael, and Terence R. Murphy. *Sleepless Souls: Suicide in Early Modern England*. Oxford: Clarendon Press, 1990.
Maclean, Hugh. "Orgoglio." *Spenser Encyclopedia*. Ed A. C. Hamilton et al.
Maresca, Thomas E. "Hell." *Spenser Encyclopedia*. Ed A. C. Hamilton et al.
Martin, Ellen E. "Spenser, Chaucer, and the Rhetoric of Elegy." *Journal of Medieval and Renaissance Studies* 17 (1987): 83-109.
McCabe, Richard A. *The Pillars of Eternity: Time and Providence in 'The Faerie Queene.'* Dublin: Irish Academic Press, 1989.
McLane, Paul E. *Spenser's Shepheardes Calender: A Study in Elizabethan Allegory*. Notre Dame, Ind.: University of Notre Dame Press, 1961.
Mogan, Joseph J., Jr. *Chaucer and the Theme of Mutability*. The Hague: Mouton, 1969.
Monsarrat, Gilles D. *Light from the Porch: Stoicism and English Renaissance Literature*. Paris: Didier Erudition, 1984.
Montrose, Louis. "'The perfect paterne of a poete': The Poetics of Courtship in *The Shepheardes Calender*." Hadfield, ed., 30-63.
Morford, Mark. *Stoics and Neostoics*. Princeton, N.J.: Princeton University Press, 1991.
Neill, Michael. *Issues of Death: Mortality and Identity in English Tragedy*. Oxford: Clarendon Press, 1997.
Nelson, William, ed. *Form and Convention in the Poetry of Edmund Spenser*. New York: Columbia University Press, 1961.
___. *The Poetry of Edmund Spenser: A Study*. New York and London: Columbia University Press, 1963.
The New Oxford Book of English Verse, 1250-1950. See Helen Gardner (Primary Sources).

Oram, William A. "Daphnaida and Spenser's Later Poetry." *Spenser Studies* 2 (1981): 141-58.

———. "*Daphnaïda.*" *Spenser Encyclopedia*. Ed A. C. Hamilton et al.

———. "Spenserian Paralysis." *Studies in English Literature* 41.1 (2001): 49-70.

Parker, Pauline M. *The Allegory of the 'Faerie Queene.'* Oxford: Clarendon Press, 1960.

Patch, Howard R. *The Goddess Fortuna in Medieval Literature*. Cambridge, Mass.: Harvard University Press, 1927.

Patrides, C. A., and J. Wittreich, eds. *The Apocalypse in English Renaissance Thought and Literature*. Manchester: Manchester University Press, 1984.

Peter, John D. *Complaint and Satire in Early English Literature*. Oxford: Clarendon Press, 1956.

Phillips, Helen. "Structure and Consolation in the Book of the Duchess." *Chaucer Review* 16 (1982): 108-18.

Pigman, G. W. *Grief and English Renaissance Elegy*. Cambridge: Cambridge University Press, 1985.

Prioreschi, Plinio. *A History of Human Responses to Death: Mythologies, Rituals, and Ethics*. Lewiston, N.Y.: Edwin Mellen, 1990.

Rasmussen, Carl J. "'How Weak Be the Passions of Woefulness': Spenser's *Ruines of Time*." *Spenser Studies* 2 (1981): 159-81.

Roche, Thomas P., Jr. "The Menace of Despair and Arthur's Vision, *Faerie Queene* I.9." *Spenser Studies* 4 (1983): 71-92.

Rolfs, Daniel. *The Last Cross: A History of the Suicide Theme in Italian Literature*. Ravenna: Longo, 1981.

Rupprecht, Carol Schreirer. "Dreams." *Spenser Encyclopedia*. Ed. A. C. Hamilton et al.

Saunders, Jason Lewis. *Justus Lipsius: The Philosophy of Renaissance Stoicism*. New York: Liberal Arts Press, 1955.

Schmidt, A. V. C., and Nicolas Jacobs, eds. *Medieval English Romances*. 2 vols. New York: Holmes & Meier, 1980.

Schoenfeldt, Michael C. *Bodies and Selves in Early Modern England: Physiology and Inwardness in Spenser, Shakespeare, Herbert, and Milton.* Cambridge: Cambridge University Press, 1999.

Skulsky, Harold. "Despair." *Spenser Encyclopedia.* Ed. A. C. Hamilton et al.

___. "Malbecco." *Spenser Encyclopedia.* Ed. A. C. Hamilton et al.

___. "Spenser's Despair Episode and the Theology of Doubt." *Modern Philology* (Feb. 1981): 227-42.

Snyder, Susan. "The Left Hand of God: Despair in Medieval and Renaissance Tradition." *Studies in the Renaissance* 12 (1965): 18-59.

Sourvinou-Inwood, Christiane. "To Die and Enter the House of Hades: Homer, Before and After." *Mirrors of Mortality: Studies in the Social History of Death.* Whaley, ed., 15-39.

Stein, Arnold. *The House of Death: Messages from the English Renaissance.* Baltimore: Johns Hopkins University Press, 1986.

Swanson, Robert N. *Religion and Devotion in Europe, c.1215-c.1515.* Cambridge: Cambridge University Press, 1995.

Tenenti, Alberto. *Il senso della morte e l'amore della vita nel Rinascimento.* Rev. ed. Torino: Einaudi, 1989.

Trevor, Douglas. *The Poetics of Melancholy in Early Modern England.* Cambridge: Cambridge University Press, 2004.

Vecchi, Linda M. "Spenser's *Complaints*: Is the Whole Equal to the Sum of Its Parts?" *Spenser at Kalamazoo.* Cleveland: Cleveland State University Press, 1984. 127-43.

Watson, Robert N. *The Rest is Silence: Death as Annihilation in the English Renaissance.* Berkeley: University of California Press, 1994.

Weatherby, Harold L. "Two Images of Mortalitie: Spenser and Original Sin." *Studies in Philology* 85 (1988): 321-52.

Webster, John and Richard Isomaki. "Pyrochles, Cymochles." *Spenser Encyclopedia.* Ed A. C. Hamilton et al.

Whaley, Joachim, ed. *Mirrors of Mortality: Studies in the Social History of Death.* London: Europe, 1981.

Whipp, Leslie T. "Weep for Dido: Spenser's November Eclogue." *Spenser Studies* 11 (1990): 17-30.

White, Lynn. "Death and the Devil." Kinsman, ed., 25-46.

Williams, Kathleen. *Spenser's World of Glass: A Reading of 'The Faerie Queene.'* Berkeley and Los Angeles: University of California Press, 1966.

Wittreich, Joseph. "Visions." *Spenser Encyclopedia*. Ed A. C. Hamilton et al.

Wrigley, E. A., and R. S. Schofield. *The Population History of England, 1541-1871: A Reconstruction*. Cambridge: Cambridge University Press, 1981.

Wymer, Rowland. *Suicide and Despair in the Jacobean Drama*. Brighton: Harvester, 1986.

Index

Abbot, George 29, 68, 69, 75, 76n
Achilles 13
Aesculapius 92-93
Alcione 115
Alcyon: as death-wisher 133-34; displaying impatience 123-27, 130; holding earthly perspectives 128-29; as obsessive griever 115; prey to self-pity and melancholy 114; self-centred 116-17; mentioned 82, 84, 86, 87, 88, 102, 105, 113, 138, 143, 163, 164
Allen, Don Cameron 26-27
Alma 90
Amavia 67, 81, 118, 119, 122, 123, 124, 130, 134n
Ambrosia 134
Anderson, Ruth L. 139n
Antiquitez de Rome (Du Bellay) 153
Aragnoll 145
Archimago 49, 82
Ariès, Philippe 1n; *Hour of Our Death* 9n, 24; *Western Attitudes* 9n, 24
Arlo Hill 152
Artegall 152
Arthur: and Pyrochles 80; and Redcrosse 38, 46, 56, 82; and Una 119, 132
Astrophel (Spenser) 130
August (eclogue in *Shep. Cal.*) 142
Augustine 22n, 40, 64, 85; *City of God* 19n, 85n

Babb, Lawrence 36n, 43n, 47n, 58n, 104n, 115n, 139n
Babe (character in *FQ*; also named Ruddymane) 122-23
Batman, Stephen 26n
Beaty, Nancy Lee 54n, 23n
Becon, Thomas 67, 69; *Dialogue* 41, 54, 62, 63; *Sicke mannes salue* 10n, 23n, 25, 54, 57n, 59, 62, 105, 125n, 129; *Solace* 125n
Beecher, Donald A. 40n, 42, 50n, 53n
Bellamy, Jane 1n
Belphoebe 81-83
Bereavement: and Alcyon 113-35; and Calidore 132n; in Spenser's works 107, 116-17; and Una 130-32
Berger, Harry, Jr. 96n, 103, 107n, 143, 145n
Bion (*Lament for Adonis*) 100
Boccaccio (*De casibus virorum illustrium*) 140
Boethius 127, 163, 165; *De consolatione philosophiae* (*The Consolation of Philosophy*) 18, 76, 125
Bonaventura, Saint 40
Book of the Duchess (Chaucer) 112, 115
Bradford, John 65
Britomart 118, 119, 150, 153, 160
Bultmann, Rudolf C. 13n, 19n
Bultot, Robert 22n
Burton, Robert 24, 104n, 111n, 138
Busirane 119

Calidore 71, 132n, 145, 151
Calvin, John 9, 20, 28n, 40, 61n, 70n, 85n, 106, 124n, 146, 156
Catullus 14n
Chaucer, Geoffrey 144; *Book of the Duchess* 112, 115; *Pardoner's Tale* 59
Cheney, Donald 3n, 92n, 134n
Cheney, Patrick 1n
Cherniss, Michael D. 125n
Cicero, Marcus Tullius, 14, 15n; *De Senectude* 61; *Tusculan Questions* 16, 115n

Clarion 138, 140, 145
Cleopolis 33, 151
Colin: his complaint in *Shep. Cal.* 142-46; as elegist in "November" 100-08; mentioned 82, 84, 112, 138
Colin Clouts (Spenser) 135n
Complaint: Colin's 142-46; Spenser's use of the literary form of 137, 139-41; Verlame's 147-49, 154-55
Complaints (Spenser) 135, 140, 141, 145, 147, 157
Contemplation (character in *FQ*) 7, 32, 33, 71, 72, 75, 88n, 92, 97, 123, 160
Contemptus mundi motif 21-22
Coverdale, Myles 69, 106n
Crampton, Georgia Ronan 62n, 81n
Cressy, David 1n
Cuddie 111n, 142
Culex 140
Cymoent 117
Cynthia 162

Daphnaida (Spenser): compared to "November" 97-100, 104, 109, 110, 115; the narrator: centrality of 113-14, compared to Alcyon 119-20, sympathetic 117-18; Spenser's rhetorical strategy 110-13, 126, 127, 129, 132; mentioned 96, 99, 137, 138, 143
Daphne: bliss 127-28; as champion of patience 126, 129-30, 134; dying speech 133; mentioned 88, 116, 117, 118
David 47
Death: desirable as end to human suffering 59-60; desirable as prevention of further sinning 64-65; fear of: in classical antiquity 15-18, in the early modern period 23-25; obsession with 9-10; views of: in Christian theology 19-23, 25, in classical antiquity 12-14
Death-wish: Alcyon's 133-34; Colin's 106; condemnation of: in Christian theology 20, 70, 75, in Spenser's work 30-31, 34-37; Phedon's 76-78; Pyrochles' 78-80; Redcrosse's 32, 36, 38, 45, 65-70, 72-73; Timias's 81-83
December (eclogue in *Shep. Cal.*) 138, 142, 143, 144, 146
Dee, John 57n
Despair (character in *FQ*): and Redcrosse 56-69; mentioned 20, 38, 44, 45, 49, 50, 51, 52, 53, 54, 55, 77, 89, 91n, 93
Despair: Alcyon's immurement in 114-15; Colin's 142-46; as devilish temptation 57-58; experienced by Redcrosse 45-48; in morality plays 54; Protestant views of 39-44, 68-69; recurrent theme in Spenser's work 6-7, 30, 33, 86-87, 120-21, 127
Dido 101-07
Dollimore, Jonathan 1n, 24n
Donne, John 85
Douglas Howard, Lady (Daphne in *Daphnaida*) 109, 129
Du Bellay, Joachim 141, 153
Duessa 44, 45, 63, 92, 93, 158
Dwarf (character in *FQ*) 131

E. K. 100n, 101, 107
Ecclesiastes 147-49
Empedocles 12
Enright, Dennis J. 29n
Epaphroditus 10n, 34n, 62, 105, 129
Epicurus 12
Erasmus, Desiderius 105, 147
Escobedo, Andrew 94n

Faerie Queene 3, 31, 33, 36, 37, 38, 61, 74, 76, 78, 82, 84, 86, 92, 118, 119, 120, 122, 126, 131, 137, 138, 152, 153, 156, 157, 158
Falls of Princes (Lydgate) 140
Fidelia 70
Fidessa 46, 93
Fig for Momus (Thomas Lodge) 141
Foucault, Michel 24n
Fowler, Alastair D. S. 123n
Furor (character in *FQ*) 77

General Index to the Publications of the Parker Society 21n, 39n
Gittings, Clare 1n
Gordon, Bruce 1n
Gorges, Arthur (Alcyon in *Daphnaida*) 109n
Graces 151, 155
Grant, Patrick 31
Grantorto 152
Guyon: and Ruddymane 122-23, and Phedon 77-78; mentioned 74, 81, 118, 119, 160

Hades 13, 87
Hamilton, A. C. 48, 61n, 62n, 81, 92n, 94, 122n, 123n, 131n
Hankins, John Erskine 101
Harris, Duncan 98n, 101, 112n, 117n, 119n, 120n
Harris, Victor 26n
Harvey, Gabriel 100n, 153
Hawkins, Sherman 162
Hazard, Mark 124n
Heale, Elizabeth 70n, 109n
Hellenore 94
Heraclitus 12
Hobbinol 144
Hoeniger, David F. 92n, 93n, 139n
Homer 15, 87
Horace 15, 16n

Houlbrooke, Ralph A. 1n, 24n, 54n, 99n
House of Holiness 36, 69, 93-94
House of Pride 45
Howard, Donald R. 22n
Hume, Anthea 73n
Hyde, Thomas 150n
Hymne of Loue (Spenser) 95n

Impermanence of human endeavours 148-49, 152-57
Irena 152
Isomaki, Richard 79n, 80n

January (eclogue in *Shep. Cal.*) 138, 143
Jeremy 41
Job 41, 47, 124
Jonah 47
Jove 159
June (eclogue in *Shep. Cal.*) 144

Kay, Dennis 99, 128n
Kerrigan, John 140n
Koller, Kathrine 23n, 55n, 60n, 86
Kristeva, Julia 89, 107n, 111n

Lambert, Ellen Z. 99n
Latimer, Hugh 28n, 33
Laurent, Alain 24n
Leicester, Robert Dudley earl of 149, 153, 154
Lipsius, Justus 17, 75, 127, 163n
Living Death: experienced by Alcyon 84, 86, 88, Colin 84, Malbecco 83, 84, 93-96, Maleger 84, 90-91, 93-94, Phedon 88, Pyrochles 79, Redcrosse 37, 86, 87, 88, Sansjoy 92-94, Timias 82, 87; motif of in Spenser's work 85-89; reversal of meanings of life and death in Spenser's work 84-86

Lobbinol 103
Lucretius 12, 16 (*De Rerum Natura*)
Luther, Martin 40
Lyons, Bridget Gellert 47n, 55n, 112n

MacDonald, Michael 44n
Machabyas Childe 117n
Maclean, Hugh 46n
Magnyfycence (also spelled *Magnificence*, Skelton) 54, 68
Malbecco 83, 84, 93, 94-96
Maleger 83, 84, 88, 89, 90-91, 93-94
Malengin 82
Mammon 73
Mankind 54
Maresca, Thomas E. 88n
Marinell 117, 157, 164
Marot, Clément: *Complainct de Madame Loyse de Savoie* 101; *Eclogue au Roy* 143
Marshall, Peter 1n
Martin, Ellen E. 112n
McCabe, Richard A. 41, 91n, 115n, 140n
McLane, Paul E. 143n
Melancholy: in the Renaissance 25-27; Spenser's use of contemporary discourses of 138-40
Melpomene 102
Merlin 160
Mogan, Joseph J. 14, 15, 19, 22n
Montrose, Louis 143n
Mordant 123
Morford, Mark 17n
Mornay, Philippe du Plessis 89n
Moschus (*Lament for Bion*) 100, 101
Mount of Contemplation 69-70, 106
Mourning: Elizabethan views of rational and godly expressions of 99, 104-07
Muiopotmos (Spenser) 138, 140, 145
Murphy, Terence R. 44n
Muses (characters in *Teares*) 100, 112,
155, 138, 155
Mutabilitie (character in *FQ*) 158-60, 162-66
Mutabilitie Cantos: 158-66; mentioned 7, 94, 130, 150, 152, 157
Myrroure for Magistrates, A 140

Napier, Richard 57
Nature (character in *FQ*) 160, 161, 162, 163, 165
Neill, Michael 1n, 24n
New Jerusalem 32, 33
November (eclogue in *Shep. Cal.*): Christian ideology of 101-06; compared to *Daphnaida* 97-100, 104, 109, 110, 115; conforming to the conventions of classical pastoral eclogues 100-01; mentioned 127, 131, 144

Odysseus 13
Oram, William A.: "*Daphnaïda*" 115n, 117n; "*Daphnaida* and Spenser's later poetry" 109n, 112n, 114n; "Spenserian Paralysis" 94n
Order (character in *FQ*) 161
Orgoglio: and his dungeon 37, 38, 47, 48, 51, 56, 77, 79, 82, 86, 87; mentioned 45, 67, 68

Paridell 94
Parker, Pauline 95n, 159
Pastoral elegy 99-101
Patch, Howard R. 127n
Patience (character in *FQ*) 70
Patrides, C. A. 26n, 88n
Paul, Saint 72
Pembroke, countess of 155
Penance (character in *FQ*) 70
Perkins, William, 69; *Salve* 23n; *Whole Treatise* 20, 43, 47, 125n, 139n
Peter, John D. 140n

Petrarch 141
Phedon 30, 76-78, 79, 81, 83
Phillips, Helen 112n
Pigman, G. W. 10, 99n, 101n, 104n, 113, 128
Plato 12, 13, 17, 21
Prioreschi, Plinio 23
Prosopopoia (Spenser) 141
Proteus 82, 158
Puttenham, George 140
Pyrochles 30, 78-81
Pythagoras 12, 61

Raleigh, Sir Walter 81n
Redcrosse: as death-wisher 36-38; and Despair 55-68; and the Dragon 72-74; in the House of Holiness 69-70, 92-93; on the Mount of Contemplation 31-32, 70-72; in Orgoglio's dungeon 45-48; and Trevisan 48-53; mentioned 7, 20, 30, 33, 34, 39, 44, 54, 75, 76, 77, 78, 79, 81, 82, 83, 86, 87, 89, 106, 119, 130, 131, 139, 151, 160
Roche, Thomas P., Jr. 57n
Rolfs, Daniel 43n
Ruddymane (named also Babe) 123
Ruines of Rome (Spenser) 141
Ruines of Time (Spenser) 147-56; mentioned 121, 138, 140, 141, 165

Sansfoy 44
Sansjoy 44, 83, 92-94
Saunders, Jason Lewis 17n
Scaliger, Julius Caesar 101
Schoenfeldt, Michael C. 1n, 90n
Schofield, R. S. 10n
Schreirer, Carol 150n,
Scudamour 118, 119
Segni, Lotario dei, Cardinal (*De miseria humanae conditionis*)

22n, 141
Seneca 11n, 17, 18, 75, 133
Shakespeare, William: *As You Like It* 115n; *King Lear* 121n; *Measure for Measure* 25n; *Sonnets* 29
Sheol 13
Shepheardes Calender (Spenser) 82, 97, 138, 141, 142, 145
Sidney, Sir Philip 116, 154
Skelton, John (*Magnificence*) 54, 62, 67
Skulsky, Harold 55n, 61n, 95n
Snyder, Susan 40n, 49n, 55n
Sourvinou-Inwood, Christiane 12, 13, 14n, 15
Southwell, Robert 10
Spenser Encyclopedia, The 1n
Spenser Review, The 1
Steele Glas (George Gascoigne) 141
Steffen, Nancy L. 98n, 101, 112n, 117n, 119n, 120n
Stein, Arnold 1n
Stella (in Spenser's *Astrophel*) 130
Strode, George 66n, 85
Suffering as common lot of humans 121-23
Swanson, Robert N. 40n
Sym, John 58, 64, 75
Sympathy for grievers: in *Daphnaida* 118; in *Faerie Queene* 118-19

Tantalus 93
Teares of the Muses 121, 138, 141, 155
Tenenti, Alberto 9n
Terwin 49, 50, 52, 58, 59, 66
Theatre...worldlings (Jan van der Noodt) 147
Thenot 100, 107
Theocritus (*Ydyll*) 100
Thomas Aquinas, Saint 40, 132n
Timias 30, 81-83, 87, 114, 135
Tree of Life 74
Trevisan 48-53

Trevor, Douglas 138n

Una: abandoned by Redcrosse 44, 49, 63; her supposed bereavement 76, 119, 130-133; in the House of Holiness 69, 70, 93; stops Redcrosse's suicidal hand 53, 67, 68; mentioned 34, 38, 45, 47, 48, 59, 82

Verlame (also spelled Verulame) 116, 138, 147-155
Virgil (Fifth *Eclogue*) 100
Virgils Gnat (Spenser) 140
Vision: Spenser's use of the topos in *Ruines of Time* and *FQ* 150-52; in *Ruines of Time* 31-33, 154, 156-57, 160-61
Visions of Bellay, The (Spenser) 153
Visions of the Worlds Vanitie, The (Spenser) 141

Watson, Robert N. 1n, 9n, 24n, 27n
Weatherby, Harold L. 90n, 122n
Webster, John 79n, 80n
Well of Life 73, 74
White, Lynn 9n, 27n
Whythorne, Thomas 39n, 63
Williams, Kathleen 52n
Wittreich, Joseph 26n, 88n, 150n
Wright, Thomas 25n, 57
Wrigley, E. A. 10n
Wymer, Rowland 43n

Ywain and Gawain 82n

Zitner, Sheldon P. 161n

STUDIES IN ENGLISH LITERATURES

Edited by Koray Melikoğlu

ISSN 1614-4651

1   *Özden Sözalan*
    The Staged Encounter
    Contemporary Feminism and Women's Drama
    2nd, revised editon
    ISBN 3-89821-367-6

2   *Paul Fox (ed.)*
    Decadences
    Morality and Aesthetics in British Literature
    ISBN 3-89821-573-3

3   *Daniel M. Shea*
    James Joyce and the Mythology of Modernism
    ISBN 3-89821-574-1

4   *Paul Fox and Koray Melikoğlu (eds.)*
    Formal Investigations
    Aesthetic Style in Late-Victorian and Edwardian Detective Fiction
    ISBN 978-3-89821-593-0

5   *David Ellis*
    Writing Home
    Black Writing in Britain Since the War
    ISBN 978-3-89821-591-6

6   *Wei H. Kao*
    The Formation of an Irish Literary Canon in the Mid-Twentieth Century
    ISBN 978-3-89821-545-9

7   *Bianca Del Villano*
    Ghostly Alterities
    Spectrality and Contemporary Literatures in English
    ISBN 978-3-89821-714-9

8   *Melanie Ann Hanson*
    Decapitation and Disgorgement
    The Female Body's Text in Early Modern English Drama and Poetry
    ISBN 978-3-89821-605-5

9   *Shafquat Towheed (ed.)*
    New Readings in the Literature of British India, c.1780-1947
    ISBN 978-3-89821-673-9

10 *Paola Baseotto*
    "Disdeining life, desiring leaue to die"
    Spenser and the Psychology of Despair
    ISBN 978-3-89821-567-1

11 *Annie Gagiano*
    Dealing with Evils
    Essays on Writing from Africa
    ISBN 978-3-89821-867-2

FORTHCOMING (MANUSCRIPT WORKING TITLES)

Lance Weldy
Seeking a Felicitous Space
The Dialectics of Women and Frontier Space in *Giants in the Earth*, *Little House on the Prairie*, and *My Antonia*
ISBN 3-89821-535-0

Kevin Cole
Levity's Rainbow
Menippean Poetics in Swift, Fielding, and Sterne
ISBN 3-89821-654-3

Pablo Armellino
Obscene Spaces in Australian Narrative
ISBN 978-3-89821-873-3

Series Subscription

Please enter my subscription to the series **Studies in English Literatures**, ISSN 1614-4651, as follows:

- ❏ complete series OR ❏ English-language titles
- ❏ German-language titles

starting with
- ❏ volume # 1
- ❏ volume # ___
  - ❏ please also include the following volumes: #___, ___, ___, ___, ___, ___,

- ❏ the next volume being published
  - ❏ please also include the following volumes: #___, ___, ___, ___, ___, ___,

- ❏ 1 copy per volume OR ❏ ___ copies per volume

Subscription within Germany:

You will receive every title on 1st publication at the regular bookseller's price incl. s & h and VAT.

Payment:
- ❏ Please bill me for every volume.
- ❏ Lastschriftverfahren: Ich/wir ermächtige(n) Sie hiermit widerruflich, den Rechnungsbetrag je Band von meinem/unserem folgendem Konto einzuziehen.

Kontoinhaber: _____ Kreditinstitut: _____
Kontonummer: _____ Bankleitzahl: _____

International Subscription:

Payment (incl. s & h and VAT) in advance for
- ❏ 10 volumes/copies (€ 319.80)   ❏ 20 volumes/copies (€ 599.80)
- ❏ 40 volumes/copies (€ 1,099.80)

Please send my books to:

NAME _____ DEPARTMENT _____
ADDRESS _____
POST/ZIP CODE _____ COUNTRY _____
TELEPHONE _____ EMAIL _____

date/signature _____

Please fax to: **0511 / 262 2201 (+49 511 262 2201)**
or mail to: *ibidem*-Verlag, Julius-Leber-Weg 11, D-30457 Hannover,Germany
or send an e-mail: ibidem@ibidem-verlag.de

***ibidem*-Verlag**
Melchiorstr. 15
D-70439 Stuttgart
info@ibidem-verlag.de

www.ibidem-verlag.de
www.ibidem.eu
www.edition-noema.de
www.autorenbetreuung.de

www.ingramcontent.com/pod-product-compliance
Lightning Source LLC
Chambersburg PA
CBHW051644230426
43669CB00013B/2436